HEIR TO THE

THRONE

THE NEW LEADER'S PATH TO
GREATNESS

AARON BAKER

Advantage®

Published by Advantage, Charleston, South Carolina.
Member of Advantage Media Group.

ADVANTAGE is a registered trademark, and the Advantage colophon is a trademark of Advantage Media Group, Inc.

Printed in the United States of America.

10 9 8 7 6 5 4 3 2 1

ISBN: 978-1-59932-770-9
LCCN: 2017947229

Cover design by George Stevens.
Layout design by Katie Biondo.

This publication is designed to provide accurate and authoritative information in regard to the subject matter covered. It is sold with the understanding that the publisher is not engaged in rendering legal, accounting, or other professional services. If legal advice or other expert assistance is required, the services of a competent professional person should be sought.

Advantage Media Group is proud to be a part of the Tree Neutral® program. Tree Neutral offsets the number of trees consumed in the production and printing of this book by taking proactive steps such as planting trees in direct proportion to the number of trees used to print books. To learn more about Tree Neutral, please visit **www.treeneutral.com.**

Advantage Media Group is a publisher of business, self-improvement, and professional development books. We help entrepreneurs, business leaders, and professionals share their Stories, Passion, and Knowledge to help others Learn & Grow. Do you have a manuscript or book idea that you would like us to consider for publishing? Please visit advantagefamily.com or call **1.866.775.1696.**

To my amazing children—Olivia, Grace, Abigail, Jack, and Jillian— who have provided me daily opportunities to learn, grow, and be a better person. I hope this gives you a road map for the journey ahead. I love you, unconditionally, forever!

ACKNOWLEDGMENTS

I must first and foremost acknowledge my mother and father, who taught me the foundational principles of life and hard work. I don't know if it was always planned, but you gave me every teaching necessary not only to survive, but to thrive. I want to thank my five beautiful children, Olivia, Grace, Abigail, Jack, and Jillian, who inspire me, support me, and push me to be my best! My first three are triplets, and at about two a.m. one night in February, 2000, these three little girls showed me that if I could work and care for them day after day, then I could do anything! That night was a pivotal point in my life.

I have to thank all the men and women who have worked with me over the years at Cannon Safe and GunVault. There are so many, but a few I must mention by name are: Steve Hoffa, who has been there to take on whatever mountain I set my sights on; Jesse Bugarin, who has been my friend since we were eighteen, working on the "docks" and gone out to battle at my side more times than I can count; Ernesto Espinoza, who gave me faith in our team when things looked the darkest. To Juan Romero, whose optimism and smile have always made me feel like we could do anything. Thank you to my work family!

This book would not be possible without hundreds of people who influenced my life, and I won't try to mention them all, but a few are: my sixth grade teacher, Mrs. Chiquita Hiyoshida, who taught me, a boy who couldn't read well, not only to read but how to find great joy in reading; and the Boy Scouts of America, who guided me through my Eagle Scout and all the lessons learned there.

To George Reyes, who has been a great legal advisor and, more importantly, a good friend.

To Ed Antillon from SCE, who has been the sounding board over so many discussions about work, employees, and life. Ed, you are the definition of a perfect friend.

I must thank everyone at Hirayama Co. in Nagoya, Japan (Mr. Zenji Kosaka, Mr. Mitsuru Fujii, Mr. Susumu Minegishi), for spending hundreds of hours with a clueless American and helping me understand deeply Kaizen and Genchi Genbutsu. A special thanks to Mami Takeda from Hirayama Co. for always seeking out new opportunities for me to learn in Japan. (See: www.genbakaizen.com)

I must thank YPO Las Vegas and especially my forum brothers Weston Adams, Darin Feinstein, Justin Kalb, Eric Kurtzman, and Todd Spector. The love, support, and accountability you provide is priceless!

My dear friend Bill Lew—I want to thank you for being a great friend, business partner, and, most of all, honest in your advice and friendship.

To Chad Fotheringham from Ecuador—as nineteen-year-old boys, to Utah, to California, through business changes, job losses, twelve kids between us, a divorce, and thousands of hours spent working through life's challenges, you have always been a true friend and confidant!

And last but not least, to my best friend and partner in all things, Vicky Nguyen. Thank you for being patient, loving, and always making me feel loved and in number-one position. You taught me at the age of forty-four what real love looks like, which is the greatest knowledge of all.

My education has been made up of hard work, trial and error, and, of course, reading! The following books (along with countless others) have had great influence on me and helped me form the secret sauce and guiding core values found in this book, so thank you to the following authors:

Mastering the Rockefeller Habits	Verne Harnish
The Mission, The Men, and Me	Peter Blaber
The Toyota Way	Jeffery Liker
The Shingo Model	Robert Miller
Start with Why	Simon Sinek
Turn the Ship Around	L. David Marquet

TABLE OF CONTENTS

PREFACE

FOR NEW LEADERS

"My job is not to be easy on people. My job is to take these great people we have and to push them and make them even better."

STEVE JOBS

I bend metal for a living. When people ask me what I do for a living, that is how I usually reply. Why?

I want to know why they ask. Are they interested in me? Is it because they just saw me get off my Gulfstream jet? Is it because they see me skiing at the only private ski resort in the world? Or, maybe, they heard I have over one thousand employees. It doesn't matter, as I never, ever set out to have this life or expected to have this success. I never woke up and told myself I was going to be a multimillionaire. I never once made a business decision strictly on money. I always made business decisions because, right or wrong, I believed it would better the lives of my team, was a cool idea, or could strengthen the growth of the company. It isn't sexy or glamorous, I know, but I chose that path over being a salesman, lawyer, or tax accountant (yes, all things I considered).

I have worked around metal on and off since I was five years old. My dad had a small welding and tools supply shop in Southern California and later went to work for a sheet metal fabrication job shop where he rose from salesman to president. It is hard, dirty, and manly work. It requires sweat, muscle, and passion. It's a long story about how I got into metal, but suffice it to say that I own a company today that bends metal into shapes and creates a residential security safe out of raw materials, with 98 percent of the safe built under one roof. We are a start-to-finish manufacturer. As a manufacturing worker by trade, I absolutely love to see raw materials transformed into a finished good. That's my story, but my story isn't exactly what this book is about.

Heir to the Throne is about the lessons I learned along that way, as I cut, bent, and shaped my path from new leader to company greatness. Now I have the opportunity to now share those lessons with you, so you can do it better.

Writing this book has been one of the hardest things I've ever done. I wrote it after years of my fellow coworkers asking me to put down in words the story, experiences, and trials that built my company and its ridiculously strong culture. I write it so they can share all of the hard things my coworkers and I have gone through with their friends and family. I love my coworkers more than I can explain. They have had my back when *no one* else did. They allowed me to roll the dice and gamble, because I knew they were amazing people.

I am not comfortable talking about the success I enjoy, because I don't want it to come off as bragging. Believe me. I would never brag, as I'm very aware of all the mistakes I have made and all the mistakes I keep making on my path of continual improvement. I also know I am a living testimony that average people can have incredible success if guided by the right core values and lots and lots of hard work.

I am humbled by the measure of success I have been blessed with and am eternally grateful for the men and women at Cannon Safe who have shared my path and taught me by example. Today, at the pinnacle of leadership as CEO and owner, I see clearly why my company has been successful, and I know what it took to become a leader so many amazing people can rely on for their livelihood. My company is not perfect and we still have a long journey ahead, but we are committed in our path to greatness.

AVERAGE PEOPLE CAN HAVE INCREDIBLE SUCCESS IF GUIDED BY THE RIGHT CORE VALUES AND LOTS AND LOTS OF HARD WORK.

I wrote this book because, as I ascended to the throne, as it were, I didn't have anyone to mentor me or tell me what I needed to do. So, I had to come up with our secret sauce by trial and error. To be honest, there have been more lonely nights than I care to remember. The weight of leadership was so heavy at times, I thought it might crush me. I have felt afraid and alone many times in my career. I hope I can be a voice of reassurance and calmness to new leaders who are feeling this same way. When I was the little guy, just starting out, I didn't know it was normal to have the feelings I did. So let me tell you: It is okay to have doubts. In fact, you'll encounter plenty of doubts on the path to greatness, and doubts are good if they drive you to learn and overcome them. As long as you are committed to staying on the path, I promise that you will enjoy success and achieve greatness.

DISCLAIMER

I am not a nice person. Nice is fake. Nice says you look great when you don't. Nice gives participation awards to everyone so they all feel warm and fuzzy inside. But the world is not nice! It is a hard, cruel place, and I want you to survive and thrive. So, because I love people and enjoy deep personal relationships, I am *kind* to all around me. To be kind means to be honest and help those around you—to encourage, motivate, and walk alongside them while not blowing smoke, sugar coating, or telling white lies. This book is *kindness.*

The stories and events in this book are all true, as they happened to me and are told from my perspective. I have changed names and a few details to protect the identity of others. I hope this book can help you on your path.

INTRODUCTION

A TRUE STORY

A few winters ago, my children and I took my private jet to go skiing in Montana. After we landed, we drove through the Rocky Mountains to reach the private resort. Snow was falling, and we were excited about the days ahead. This is my son's reality—private jets, fancy resorts, wonderful holidays with Dad—but I'm well aware that it's not most kids' realities. It certainly wasn't my reality when I was his age. When you're a kid, though, you take for granted whatever you're used to.

As I drove, we were talking about the skiing we'd be doing later in the day when I remembered that I had to be on a conference call. "Sorry, Jack," I said. "We'll have to wait to hit the slopes until I'm off the call."

His look of disappointment made me add, "Jack, I think maybe it's time for me to retire. I'm not sure I can take the company any further than I've taken it—and I think there are other things I need to focus on in life."

I didn't say this merely in response to his disappointment. I was going through some self-doubt at the time, reassessing my life and what I wanted to do with it. Meanwhile, I think Jack had been going through his own period of self-awareness and questioning. Despite the fact that he had grown up in an affluent family where he had never had to face much danger or hardship, his perfect life had been shattered when his mom and I got divorced. This was the first true challenge he'd had to face, and it had woken him up to adulthood. It nudged his consciousness up a notch or two, to a place with a view of the world that challenged his nine-year-old eyes.

And so he started asking questions I'd never heard him ask before: "How does life work? What am I going to do for a living? Will my life look like yours, Dad? What will I spend all my time doing? What profession or business will I get into? Who will I marry?" (He's nine years old, for Pete's sake! Why is he worried about getting married?) Maybe he was looking to put the world back on solid footing after his mom and I had shaken it so badly. Whatever his reasons, I was glad he felt he had the power to take control of his life, even if he still didn't know all the answers.

This was where he was coming from, on that day, and as we drove to the ski resort, he said to me, "I don't want you to retire, Dad."

"Jack," I said, "do you understand that for most of my life, my work has been my life? I've spent more hours working than I've spent doing anything else. I've spent more hours building my career than any other thing in my life—more than being a dad, more than being a husband, more than being a friend." As I said, I was deep in self-doubt. My work was all-consuming. I was feeling, at the time, ready to hang it up. The question I kept asking myself was whether my work was really worth what it was doing to the rest of my life.

Because I'd expected Jack to be overjoyed at the thought I might have more time to spend with him, I was surprised by his reaction. "Why wouldn't you want me to stop working so much?" I asked him. "Wouldn't you like me to have more time to have fun with you and your sisters, instead of always having to work?"

He shook his head. "No, Dad."

"Well, why not?"

"Because," he said, "I want to be part of your work. I want to be the heir to the throne."

There I was, thinking it was time to be done with work, while he wanted to get started. The contrast between our two perspectives was so sharp that I took my eyes off the road to look at him. I opened my mouth to say something but shut it again and turned my attention back to my driving.

What I'd been about to say was this: "Oh my gosh! You don't even know what you're talking about! It's crazy to even think about it. You couldn't ever be the heir to this. It's too big already. It's so far ahead of you. How would you ever catch up?" I caught back my words in time, though.

We drove along in silence for a few miles, and all the while I was thinking, *He is my son. Are his ideas really completely off base? Maybe he could. I don't know.* The snow kept falling, and my thoughts kept going: *You're his dad. It would be up to you to teach him what he needs to know. But if he really wants to be the heir to the throne, do you have any idea how to prepare him to be that? How could you teach him?*

Something inside me shifted and clicked into place. I had an overwhelming feeling that I had accepted a new challenge. *Okay, my son wants to be the heir to the throne. How am I going to teach him how*

3

to run a company? I didn't have the answer yet, but I did know this: A lot of hard work would have to take place first if he were going to do it, and he would have to learn a lot of things.

I knew that I, by far, didn't know everything. Even with all my experience, I still make mistakes. But I also knew that we learn through our mistakes. So some things my son would have to learn through his own experience, but, maybe, there were other things I could teach him so that when he was ready to begin, he would have a head start. He wouldn't have to repeat the same mistakes I'd made, because he could learn from *my* experience.

All this time, we'd both been staring through the windshield at the falling snow, thinking our own thoughts. Now, he said, "Dad, I want to start sweeping the floors and working my way up."

I don't know where he came up with that idea, and I had to laugh, but that's exactly how I'd learned the manufacturing business: I started at the grunt level and worked my way up. He'd probably heard me say that, sometime.

For me, that conversation on a snowy road in Montana was the beginning of a new way of thinking about my work. My son didn't forget what we'd discussed either. Just the other day, he said to me, "When can I start working, Dad?"

"Well," I said, "you turned ten yesterday, so you're still a little too young to work, but in a couple of years you can begin."

"What will I be doing?" he asked.

"I'm not sure yet, Jack," I said, "but in the meantime, I'll be teaching you everything I know about being a good business leader."

NEW LEADERS: THIS BOOK IS FOR YOU

So that's what this book is: all the things I know about leadership that I want to share with my son and any other new leader out there. If you're entering the business world—or if you've already been there for a while but are struggling to achieve something greater—I want to offer this to you as well.

When I started out, I had aspirations of learning and growing my path to success. I wanted to participate in something that I found meaningful and impactful to all those involved.

But as my son had, I also had this fairy-tale idea of what I wanted to do—and very little idea of what it would take, in reality, to make that happen. A large chasm lay between the two, and there was no way I could simply leap across it. Instead, I had to hike all the way down to the bottom before I could make my way to the top of the other side.

If you've just entered the business world or just received a promotion that puts you into a leadership position, this is an exciting moment in your life. You're excited about the money that goes along with your new title, of course, but you're also excited about the new responsibilities. At the same time, you may be scared to death of all the things for which you'll now be held accountable. (And if you're *not* scared to death, you should be!)

Do you really know what your new position will entail? Do you know what it will take to be a good leader? Here's what I can tell you: First and foremost—more than anything else—you need to be willing to define yourself by the following *ten big fundamentals*:

1. Embrace culture first.

2. Continually improve.

3. Be loyal.

4. Enjoy hard work.

5. Be sure that your actions speak louder than words.

6. Respect others (my favorite chapter).

7. Love change.

8. Yearn to learn.

9. Think of money as just a way to keep score.

10. Pay attention to just four things—and delegate the rest.

Those ten big fundamentals helped me cut, bend, and shape my path to building a self-funded, high-growth company to over $100 million. In the chapters that follow, I'll share with you what I've learned about each of one. I guarantee they'll make you a great leader, someone who not only makes money but who blesses others and is worthy of being heir to the throne.

CHAPTER 1
EMBRACE CULTURE FIRST

Whether a company has a great leader depends upon
whether its leader decides to become one. It is a decision,
it is a choice, it is a journey. It is not a birthright.

JIM COLLINS

Prior to 2010, I didn't think a whole lot about corporate culture. Sure, we had one at Cannon Safe, but we weren't very aware of it. Since the day I became CEO and owner, we had a mission statement and values, but we hadn't really defined our culture. Things at the time seemed to be working just fine in our US facility. But the same couldn't be said for our Mexican facility, so I decided to send the US leadership down to Mexico in order to make sure we all shared the same mission and strategies.

Right away, I realized I had a problem. The Mexican facility started doing better, but without the leadership team, the US facility was no longer doing as well. In fact, it was falling apart. I brought the leadership people back to the United States, and things picked up again—but the Mexican facility was right back where it started. I was frustrated that we couldn't seem to keep things on track without strong leadership on site.

I had read books about Toyota that said the leaders there have very little to do with day-to-day processes. I wondered why we couldn't be like that. What was our problem? What did Toyota have that we didn't? I knew I'd worked to give my employees the best possible tools, and we were following the most efficient processes. Yet, we still weren't operating the way we needed to. I decided to go to Japan myself so I could discover Toyota's secret sauce.

On my first day in Japan, I stopped and talked to a worker. "What's this?" I asked him, pointing to three different tools in little holders.

"Oh, those are the tools I use to adjust a part," he told me. "I used to spend half my time trying to lay my hand on the right one. I'd use one, set it down, start doing something else, and then turn around and have to look for the right tool all over again. So I came up with a solution."

He'd made color-coordinated little holders that kept his tools within arm's reach, right where he needed them when he had to grab one. I watched this guy for a long time. I realized that he'd seen a problem in his work, and he'd figured out a way to fix it, without ever asking for help from management. He truly owned his work.

Later that day, as I was being shown around by one of the managers, I pointed to another tool a worker was using and asked, "What's that?"

The manager shrugged. "I don't know. That worker there, he came up with it."

The more I listened and watched, the more I realized that these guys never even talked about the tools they used for manufacturing. Their constant focus was on their culture and their core values. Workers had that culture in their face every minute of every day, and it had become so absorbed that it was second nature to them. They weren't just following orders, the way my employees did. These people owned their work.

Slowly, painfully, I realized that everything I'd been focusing on as a leader revolved around the tools we used. I had put tools in place to improve efficiency, increase production, facilitate work, reduce unnecessary physical movement, and eliminate waste. I thought I'd been doing all the right things, but I'd never encouraged my employees to ask questions about how the job could be done better (even though I should have realized that the people actually doing the work would have valuable insights). I might as well have been working with robots!

I found myself remembering something that happened to me when I was starting out as a grunt worker in a fabrication shop. A supervisor came in and told me to de-burr about a hundred thousand parts.

"Okay," I said.

"Here's how you do it," he told me. "You're going to take twenty-five parts, throw them into the machine, run them in the machine for five minutes, stop the machine. Take those twenty-five parts out. Take twenty-five more parts, put them in, turn on the machine . . . and that's what you're going to do until they're all de-burred."

I did it exactly the way he told me to do it. The whole job took me a long time, at least a couple weeks. It was horrendously boring, standing there in front of the machine, wearing ear protection against the loud vibrations, hour after hour, day after day. But I did it.

My supervisor left his position a little while later. When the same de-burring job came up again, my new supervisor looked at the paperwork and said to me. "So you've done this job before. Can you do it again?"

"Sure," I said, though my heart sank at the idea.

The supervisor looked down at the paper in his hand. "Looks like it took you a long time last time."

"Yeah," I said. "It did."

"Why?"

"I don't know," I told him. "It's just a lot of parts to get through."

He looked at me. "Well, do you think we're doing it the right way?"

"What?" Nobody had ever asked me a question like that.

"Are we doing it the right way?" he repeated.

I'd never given a thought to the process. I'd just been doing what I was told. Finally, I said, "I don't know. I guess I'd need to know why we have to do this. What are we hoping to accomplish?"

The guy looked at the paper again, and then he shrugged. "I really don't know."

So we asked an engineer why the job needed to be done. He told us, "When someone uses this product, we don't want this edge to be sharp. It might cut someone."

"Okay," I said. "So we just have to make it so a human hand can touch it and not be cut?"

"That's right."

He watched while I starting going through the parts, touching them with my fingertips. I found that a lot of them were already pretty close to that standard.

I said to him, "Do I have to throw them all in the machine and run them for five minutes?"

He shook his head. "They just have to not be sharp. You can do it however you want."

Now that I understood the reason for what I was doing, I came at the job from an entirely new perspective. I was no longer just obeying orders. I developed a system for sorting through the parts. Some of them didn't need any de-burring, some of them needed a minute or so in the machine, and only a few needed the full five minutes I'd been giving them all. I'd asked why, and I'd gotten an answer that allowed me to figure out what was truly the best way to do the work. I finished the entire job in three days.

Every single day, Toyota leaders encourage their workers to ask why. As a result, their workers are fully invested in what they do. They come at their job with curiosity and enthusiasm. They don't need someone standing over them, telling them what to do. If the leadership stepped out for a week, things would continue as smoothly as ever. That's the kind of culture they have, and it saturates every aspect of the company.

If you're in a leadership position, ask yourself if you are telling people how to do things or telling them why those things need to be done. Are you giving orders, or are you encouraging the people who are closest to the work to come up with their own ideas? Are you supporting a culture where workers own their work?

Workers who own their work are more likely to enjoy their work, even the inevitably boring parts. They enjoy working hard, because they know why they're working, and they know their efforts make a difference.

Embrace culture first. Culture is what allows your people to achieve greatness, so if you're on the path to greatness, you won't get very far without culture.

KNOW YOURSELF, KNOW YOUR CULTURE

Your company's culture starts with you. That means you need to know who you are, as well. I realized this when I was about halfway into my career. I was having dinner with Abe Cubano, an old friend I've known since we were both nineteen. We'd both come a long way since those days when we were dirt poor, and now we were both established in our work, with families of our own.

As we were eating, having a good time together, Abe said to me, "Aaron, you are exactly the same person you were when you were nineteen years old."

"That's kind of rude," I said. "You mean I haven't grown at all?"

"No, I don't mean it that way. I mean that when you were nineteen, you already knew who you were. It's so interesting. I'm sitting here listening to you talk, and you're still the same guy."

EMBRACE CULTURE FIRST. CULTURE IS WHAT ALLOWS YOUR PEOPLE TO ACHIEVE GREATNESS, SO IF YOU'RE ON THE PATH TO GREATNESS, YOU WON'T GET VERY FAR WITHOUT CULTURE.

He was right. I have known who I am since I was a young man. I know that I'm kind of average-looking, not the best-looking guy in the world, but I'm okay. I'm not the smartest guy by far, to be honest with you. I was an okay student with a B average in school. I have no desire to have an entourage. I like to work hard. I'm not much of a joker. I'm not a superstar, but I'm a solid player. And yes, I knew all that when I was nineteen. I've never tried to pretend I'm someone I'm not. Those qualities have shaped my leadership. In turn, as I built my business, my personal qualities shaped my business's culture.

> *It has long been understood that our beliefs have a profound effect on our behavior. What is often overlooked, however, is the equally profound effect that systems have on behavior.*
> **SHIGEO SHINGO**

If you want to be a leader, I believe your first, most vital task is to get to know who you are. As a leader, you need to be honest with yourself. You need to know what you're good at and what you're not. My self-awareness of my strengths and weaknesses may be my most important skill as a leader. I know what I can do myself—and I know what I need to hire others to do.

Leaders also need to be honest about their companies' cultures. They need to be able to see clearly how their own qualities interact with that culture, for good or bad. That relentless honesty is necessary if you want to make your company's culture strong.

There's no point being envious of other leaders' qualities and other companies' cultures. When I've visited Zappos, for example, I see the crazy stuff they do, the fun culture they have, and I just smile. It's cool, but it's not who I am, and it's not part of the culture of the company I've built. By the same token, I know I'm not a nuclear scientist. I'm a welder. I'm a line worker by trade, someone who makes things and gets them done, and that's the sort of company I've created as well. I'm realistic about who I am, just as I'm realistic about the culture of my company.

Now don't get me wrong. I'm not saying that certain aspects of your culture can't be tweaked. Sometimes, those small adjustments are definitely necessary for the health of the business. But recognize the DNA, that deepest pattern that helped build your company in the first place, and honor it, support it, enhance it. Don't try to fight against it. Don't try to turn your company into something it's not. If you try to do that, you'll end up in trouble.

And by the same token, don't try to change yourself into something different from who you truly are. I saw this play out in the career of a former management employee—and it wasn't pretty!

My management team takes personality tests: an "adaptive" test and a "natural" test. Adaptive tests measure what you have learned during your career, while natural tests identify who you really are. We like to know both, because in times of stress and pressure, people tend to revert back to their natural state, who they are at their core. In most cases, adaptive results aren't terribly different from natural results. Most of us learn a few skills to enhance our work performance, but in general, we're still the people we've always been.

But not this manager. His test results showed him to be the complete opposite on the outside from who he was on the inside.

He appeared to be a hard-charging, take-no-prisoners type of guy. His adaptive score, however, was at the opposite end of the scale, indicating that he was a mild-mannered, meek fellow. He had forgotten who he was and was trying to be something he wasn't. He had chosen a career path that he thought required him to conform to a particular personality type—and he'd done his best to cram his true nature inside that personality, even though it was a terrible fit.

When this employee and I met with the test administrator, the administrator told him he was concerned for him as a human being. It was not good for anybody to have his adaptive state be so completely the opposite of who he really was. "When that happens," the administrator said, "I can guarantee that if you get in a high-stress situation, you'll revert back to your natural state. Everybody around you will be like, 'Who *is* this guy?' They'll think you've lost your mind—and you'll feel a huge loss of control. It will be just too drastic a swing for either you or the people around you to deal with."

A couple of years later, the test administrator's prediction proved to be accurate. We were going through a phenomenally rapid growth phase, and this guy couldn't handle the pressure. He came completely unglued, and crashed and burned. It was painful to watch, but there was nothing we could do at that point. He was no longer an effective leader of his department, and he ended up getting a couple of demotions. Eventually, he moved on to a different job—all because he didn't really know who he was. He wasn't being true to his actual identity.

At a recent presentation, the speaker, Cameron Herold, said, "We have a kid who's incredible at soccer and stinks at basketball. So what do we do? We hire a private basketball coach, and we drill, drill, drill so the kid can become a mediocre basketball player, when what we should have done was make him even better at soccer." The same principle works for us. If we know we have a weakness in a certain area, pretending isn't going to make it go away. Sure, we may be able to learn a few compensatory skills, but oftentimes, the best course of action is to focus on our strengths, the things we can do better than most people, and hire people who can fill the gaps in our own abilities.

For example, I am not a great writer. In fact, my handwriting is horrible. I don't have the patience for it. I can type fairly fast, but I still can't type as fast as I can talk or think, so it starts to seem like a waste of time. Then I begin cutting corners, not saying everything

I want to say. So what do I do to compensate for this flaw of mine? Well, if I need to draft a good, descriptive e-mail to my team, I don't write it myself. Instead, I sit down with my wonderful COO, and we talk. This guy is not a talker, the way I am, but he is a very intense listener. On top of that, he is extremely methodical and logical. So, I give my words to him. Then he drafts an e-mail. What he writes is always exactly what I want to say. Writing is not my strength, and I'm not envious that this guy can do so well what I do so poorly. Instead, I'm grateful for him. I'm glad that his talents and my talents complement each other so well. We each have our own role, and because we're true to our strengths and weaknesses, we enhance and support the entire business's culture.

As strange as it may seem at first glance, being comfortable with who you are is an essential part of being a company's cultural leader. And one skill you can and should develop is the ability to do a self-inventory.

This is something I do every Sunday. I look over the week behind me, and I ask myself how I did in the areas where I've already identified some weaknesses. So I might ask myself such questions as:

- Was I good about unplugging and focusing on my children as they talked to me—not working at the same time and giving them only half my attention?

- Did I get back to those employees who e-mailed me that they needed to talk to me? Did I stop and take time for them?

- How is the business culture doing? Are we living up to our core values? Have we strayed off the path anywhere?

As you can see, the questions I ask myself aren't necessarily work related. That's because I'm all one piece—there's no "work Aaron" and "family Aaron"—and I need to be able to integrate who I am, weaknesses and strengths, into both my family and my employees. The same qualities that help me be a good leader at work will also help me be a better father, and the more I practice these qualities, in both areas of my life, the stronger they become.

Taking time for weekly self-reflection like this is critical to being a good leader. As regularly taking a personal inventory becomes your natural way of doing things, your leadership will become more consistent. Your employees will be happier, because human beings crave consistency. As you focus on making the company culture consistent, they'll be able to do all the stuff that has to get done more effectively and at a better pace. Live by the commandment of *know thyself.*

PROTECT YOUR COMPANY CULTURE

Whenever you get people together and give them a task to do, as a team, very quickly a set of values emerges among the group. In business, we call that a corporate culture.

Every company has its own unique culture. Each group of individuals will elect to focus, as a whole, on some characteristics more than others. Their culture usually starts at the birth of the company, with maybe only five people. Those individuals bring their personal values to the company—and these values tend to stick. They become part of the company's heart and soul.

As the company grows and new hires are made, some people will be drawn naturally to its corporate culture. Others will adapt to it. Some, though, will not be comfortable with it and leave. This is an ongoing process.

Now, if you're the heir to the throne—or if you've advanced into a position of greater authority—the challenge you'll face is this: How do you keep the corporate culture alive and strong while adding to it in a way that's beneficial to everyone concerned? How do you adapt your personal values to enhance the corporate culture rather than fight against it? You'll be making a big mistake if you think you can put a new corporate culture in place that suits you better than the existing one.

> *When you're building an institution, you're consciously growing something that will be beyond you. It will exist without you, it'll grow beyond you, it'll sustain itself beyond you . . . It's about creating culture and values that persist. It's that psychic glue that holds it all together.*
> **DHARMESH SHAH, COFOUNDER OF HUBSPOT**

Let's say you're the new CEO at a company that's accustomed to being 100 percent focused on hard work. Folks there don't joke around, they don't laugh while they work, and they don't play pranks on each other. If you come in and start playing practical jokes on everyone, they'll be thrown off balance. Or, if you announce that you're going to initiate Whacky Fridays for which everyone dresses up according to a weekly theme, the whole organization will go into a tailspin. I've seen this sort of thing happen, and I've learned that drastic changes like this—massive shifts in the corporate culture—are disastrous. Companies need to protect their corporate culture. It gives them stability and helps make them strong.

When companies grow, as mine did, past the $50 million mark—and then the $75 million mark—the original executives tend to move into new roles. They become the ones who strategize the big picture, which means they've stepped back from the day-to-day fray. As new leaders step in to fill their place, those individuals need to comprehend the depth of the existing corporate culture. Before they begin, they have to truly understand the company's driving forces, the values that have shaped its culture.

If you're a corporate leader, your number-one responsibility every single day is culture, culture, culture. Culture is everything. It's a living entity that can't be ignored. If you do ignore it—if you let your culture slip—you'll run into problems. Let's say the company has always been a kick-back-and-relax company, and you decide you're going to switch to a hard-charging, take-the-hill company. I can guarantee you'll fail. That high-energy, aggressive approach just won't match up with the company's easygoing culture.

As the leader, you need to fit in with the corporate culture— and so does everyone you hire. If you start hiring a bunch of people with different values from those of your corporate culture, you'll end up diluting, and ultimately weakening, your corporate culture. I've learned this from experience, as my company grew.

We'd always been a take-no-prisoners sort of company. We held high expectations for ourselves, and we worked hard to live up to them. In the company's early days, we weren't talking much about culture, but we had one nevertheless—and it was attractive to a certain kind of person. In fact, we existed for forty years without a defined culture. We hired a lot of people with a great deal of self-confidence and not a whole lot of pedigree or education. These were seasoned workers who were comfortable inside their own skins. They knew what they were good at, and their attitude was "Hey, I don't have a college degree, but I know how to work really hard," or "I'm not the best at math, but I really understand retail sales and what retailers are looking for in the products they buy." In other words, they were hard workers with plenty of common-sense skills. They fit right in with our culture, and they thrived with us.

For the past few years, though, our culture filter has probably become a little too open. We've let some people in who don't hold the same core values as we do. Now we're tightening that up again. We have to do that, not because we're exclusionary, but because we need everyone on our team to be on the same page. We have to be a unified whole that works together, not just a bunch of people all going in different directions.

At the same time, as you work with your employees, don't get hung up on surface differences. When you get deeply involved with a group of people, you'll be able to see the commonalities you share. Don't let external categories divide you.

My friendship with a guy named Bill is a good example of differences that end up being only skin deep. At first glance, you'd think we were a pretty odd couple. He's highly educated, earned advanced degrees, and studied economics in London years ago. I'm someone who worked my way up the hard way. I attended a state school and worked full time and started a retail business while in school. Bill is also at the far left of the political spectrum, while I have to admit I'm all the way over on the right. And yet, despite those differences, he's one of my dearest friends. We can talk for hours about anything under the sun, and oddly enough, we usually find that we agree on pretty much 99 percent of everything we discuss. We've cut past all the rhetoric. We've found our common ground, the place where we share what's truly most important to us. What we share are called core values.

In a business, the company culture has to be the common ground that everyone shares, despite individual differences. The culture is what brings everyone together into an effective workforce. You can have the best technology and marketing strategies in the world, but if your culture is weak, invisible, or nonexistent, you're not going to succeed in the business world for very long.

A couple of famous sayings about this idea that have been floating around the business world for a while now:

Culture trumps strategy.

Culture eats strategy for breakfast.

Culture is what really makes or breaks a company. It's a concept that a lot of people talk about. There are books written about it. And yet, supporting a successful company culture is easier said than done.

As you step into a leadership position, you need to know this: Culture is the DNA that defines who you are as a company. It's imbedded so deeply in the company that trying to change it from the outside would be like telling your daughter to stop having her mother's eyes. You need to recognize this at a deep level. Make it your focus. Only then will you be able to build on the company's strengths.

> *Culture is simply a shared way of doing something with a passion.*
> **BRIAN CHESKY, COFOUNDER AND CEO OF AIRBNB**

BE CONSISTENT

I learned about the importance of consistency back when I was working in a state youth correctional facility. When the kids came out of long-term incarceration, they were brought to the unit where I worked. There, we did what we called observation and assessment. These teenagers were still locked up, but now they were in a smaller, more residential-looking setting. They had a kitchen, and they went to school. My job was to see if they were ready to go back into society.

What I found was that these kids thrived when they had a consistent pattern to their days. We woke them up at the same time every morning, and they went through the same routines: bathroom, breakfast, cleanup and other chores, school, lunch, activity, more school, one-on-one counseling, work details, free time, group counseling, bedtime, and lights out. You might think the daily pattern became boring, but it didn't. They knew exactly what to expect, and most of them did very well.

I was putting myself through college at the time. So, to get some extra money, I also did some work as a parole officer for juvenile delinquents. This gave me the opportunity to follow up on some of the kids who had been released from my observation unit. What I saw was that many of the kids who had done so well in a strong, structured environment fell apart when they got out into the real world, especially if they went back to their homes and families. For most of them, home meant a place with a single parent who was seldom there. There was no structure at all, no accountability or predictability. The kids were on their own—and they couldn't handle it. After I became aware of this, I never recommended that the kids in my unit be released back to their families unless I saw a very strong, consistent structure already in place in that home.

Obviously, I'm not saying that employees are like juvenile delinquents. But the fact is that none of us flourishes in chaos. I know that's true for me. I remember how it felt when the workplace was in constant pandemonium, back when I was a worker and not a corporate leader. One manager said one thing; another said something totally different. It wasn't clear to me how to do my job well. It wasn't clear to anyone!

Not only does chaos make employees unhappy, but it also makes them less productive. As leaders, then, we need to constantly ask ourselves if we are building consistency, a structured culture where all employees understand what's expected of them. Do people know what they're going to walk into when they come to work every day? If we can answer yes to those questions, then we're already well on our way to being the kind of strong leaders we need to be.

> *Connect the dots between individual roles and the goals of the organization. When people see that connection, they get a lot of energy out of work. They feel the importance, dignity, and meaning in their job.*
> **KEN BLANCHARD**

CHAPTER 2
CONTINUALLY IMPROVE

As your organization grows, you must grow as fast or faster to stay relevant. Have you ever seen the documentary film *Jiro Dreams of Sushi*? (If not, I encourage you to see it!) It's the story of an old man who owns a sushi restaurant—a tiny little place with only just a few seats and no restroom—in one of Tokyo's subway stations. There's nothing fancy about it. To be honest, it looks like a dive. But guess what? That tiny restaurant was awarded a prestigious three-star Michelin Guide rating. Sushi lovers from around the world go to the subway station just to eat Jiro's food. In fact, they call months in advance and shell out top dollars to get a coveted seat at Jiro's sushi bar.

I've eaten there a few times. There are no fancy sauces, and the food is simple, but the flavors Jiro brings out of it blow my mind every time. Jiro is truly the greatest sushi chef in the world.

When Jiro started out, I'm sure there were plenty of other sushi chefs as good as he was. He's been making sushi for sixty-some years, and he's continually improved his sushi, over and over and over, during that entire time. He watches his customers, and he constantly adjusts his food to meet their needs. If you're left-handed, for example, Jiro will notice, and your food will always be placed on the left side of your plate rather than the right. If you're a larger person, you may get a larger portion than someone who looks as if they have a smaller appetite. Jiro also notices what works best when he's preparing his food. As a result, he knows the exact pressure to use when he whisks an egg for his famous sweet-cake dessert. He pays attention to the smallest of nuances and then uses them to make his food even better. He never stops improving.

> *Without continual growth and progress, such words as improvement, achievement, and success have no meaning.*
>
> **BENJAMIN FRANKLIN**

LAURELS ARE NOT GOOD RESTING PLACES!

Growing up in Southern California, I noticed that actors who looked as if they were turning into superstars one year could totally disappear just a year or two later. Maybe they had a hit series that came to an end. Today, we may wonder what happened to so-and-so and what's-his-name. They probably felt their professional success was in the bag. They were resting comfortably on their laurels—and they woke up just a few years later in obscurity.

Jiro, the sushi chef, has never considered resting on his laurels. His entire life is focused on continually improving his performance. It's where all his passion goes. You might say that it's a goal he'll never reach, because there is no end to improvement. Perfection is a moving target. Whether you make sushi or build cars or create art, there is always, always, always room to make your work better. For Jiro, that means his entire identity is wrapped up in advancing his performance every single day. It's his reason for living.

JIRO ONO: I'LL CONTINUE TO CLIMB TO TRY TO REACH THE TOP, BUT NO ONE KNOWS WHERE THE TOP IS!

WHY ARE *YOU* HERE?

It's a simple question I often ask people who work for me or who come to me for advice: Why are you here? What is your purpose for being alive? I'm not expecting a deep, religious answer. Instead, I want people to think about the questions seriously and find the answer that's all their own.

It's a question we all need to consider, because if we don't know the answer, we don't know where to direct our efforts toward improvement. Take Jiro. He's probably not a skilled athlete or a musical virtuoso, and he doesn't waste his energy trying to be. He knows that his purpose in life is to make sushi, so that's where he focuses his attention.

Once you know what your purpose is, then continual improvement becomes much clearer. You can make it a focal point. If, for example, you're a comedian, and your purpose on earth is to make people laugh, then you apply the same principles Jiro does to sushi:

you pay attention to what makes people laugh most. You constantly refine and adjust your comic routine so that it becomes funnier and funnier. You know that you'll never wake up one morning and be able to say, "There, I made it! Now I am the funniest comedian in the world. From now on, I can just keep doing what I've been doing, for the rest of my life."

Being willing to continually improve means you're committed to growing and changing. In the documentary about Jiro's life, he says that what he loves about making sushi is that he climbs and climbs and climbs, trying to get to the summit—and when he gets there, he realizes there's a taller mountain behind the one he's on.

> *Very few people or companies can clearly articulate WHY they do WHAT they do. By WHY I mean your purpose, cause or belief—WHY does your company exist? WHY do you get out of bed every morning? And WHY should anyone care?*
> **SIMON SINEK**

SHOOT FOR THE STARS

Committing yourself to the concept of continual improvement means being determined to work for perfection while always being aware that you will never obtain perfection. That's a hard concept to swallow at first. You've probably heard the saying that goes something like this: Shoot for the moon, because even though you're bound to miss, you'll still end up out there in the stars. We're a very goal-oriented species, though, and we don't like to think we can't schedule our moon landing on a precise crater on an exact date. After all, why should we try to achieve something that we know from the start is an impossible goal?

Our society equates success with completion. Something that's never quite achieved is considered a failure, but I suspect that our lives' purposes have nothing to do with completion. It's about the journey. Forget about shooting for the moon. Instead, aim for the stars from the get-go, and prepare for a lifetime space voyage. You're never going to be "all grown up," because you can keep growing and improving until the day you die.

Sometimes, that may require making a drastic change to the way you do things. If your rocket ship is pointed straight toward an asteroid, you need to course correct, or you'll never get past that chunk of space rock. Don't beat yourself up if that happens. Most of us at one time or another have gotten so far off course in one way or another (whether in our professional or personal lives) that we have had to make a major course correction. We have to drastically revamp the way we do things—and that, generally, requires that we also totally change our attitudes and perspectives so that we can get back to journeying through the stars.

Hopefully, that kind of drastic change is required far less often than the slow, gradual change that produces continual improvement in our lives. This slower kind of change is a daily thing that is more like the minor course corrections we make on the steering wheel all the time when we're driving. It's those tiny nuanced changes that keep us on course.

KAIZEN

There's a Japanese word that perfectly describes this concept: *kaizen*. This kind of change doesn't happen all at once. You don't wake up one morning and say, "Today I'm going to never lose my temper again," or, "Today I am going to set a new personal best at weightlifting." It's usually not a huge jump that takes you from ground zero into outer space. It's one step today, another step tomorrow, and the next day, and the day after that.

Kaizen doesn't always equate with small changes, though, and it isn't simply change for change's sake. It's a daily process that brings big results from many small changes accumulated over time. Each change, no matter how small, leads toward widespread transformation.

At the organizational level, this means that kaizen involves *everyone*—but the greatest transformation is led by senior management. Your role as the leader is key to spearheading a kaizen movement that will involve every single person at your business.

The word Kaizen is Japanese and means
"CONTINUOUS IMPROVEMENT"

Kai = Change   Zen = Good

KAIZEN LEADERSHIP

If you're in a leadership position, you have responsibility for the lives of other people. It's your job to not only ensure that they have a livelihood but also to set them an example. In the course of my career,

I've found that the most important example I can set as a leader is a commitment to continual improvement.

If you look at leadership from this perspective, you'll be able to see pretty quickly that being a leader has nothing to do with being better than everyone else. It has absolutely nothing to do with competition. That may seem counterintuitive (because, after all, you may assume that you reached a leadership position by being competitive). But think about it: If your leadership is based on competition (on the fact that you've risen higher than the others around you), you'd never want your staff to grow, because you'd see their growth as a threat to your leadership. You wouldn't want them to overtake you in skills or maturity or anything else, because, then, you might no longer be the leader, right?

But that doesn't work as well as you might think. You don't really want your employees to be incompetent, do you? Your role as a leader isn't to be *better* than everyone else; it's to be the spearhead, the unifying force that points everyone toward the ongoing goal of continual improvement. This means fostering an environment where your people feel both supported and held accountable to press forward that one step each day. Collectively, this sets the entire organization on course for the stars, and individually, it means that each person becomes better and better in whatever skill set is most important to that individual.

As the leader, you expect each person to be able to answer these questions:

What are you doing to learn?

What are you doing to grow?

How are you improving?

What have you improved this week?

As a leader, you've taken a sacred responsibility upon yourself for people's careers and livelihood—and that includes everything from their children's college funds to their retirement funds, from the money for their first home to the expense of their kids' braces. This means you have a responsibility to help these people achieve their success. You do this by holding them accountable for ways in which they're going to improve, and then, when they reach that set of goals, you give them their next challenge.

SETTING YOUR BASELINE

When people resist the challenge of continual improvement, I've found that I can reframe the conversation to be less threatening by turning it around. I say, "Don't you want to make your life *easier*? Because if you can learn just one new thing, that could be the thing that will make your life go more smoothly." To do this, though, you need to establish a baseline for whatever the challenge is, because you can't improve something for which you have no basis of comparison. One of my great mentors in Japan, Mr. Fujimoto, says, "There is no kaizen where there is no standard." You need to establish what your standard is for comparison.

Let's say you pick one thing in yourself that you want to improve—and you start measuring it. If you want to run faster, you start by taking your current time for running a mile, or if you want to increase the paperwork flow across your desk, you determine the time it takes to fill out one of the standardized forms you do over and over. You will very quickly see that the second you start measuring something in your life, your brain will step in and find ways to do it more efficiently. You'll automatically kick yourself out of cruise control, and instead, you'll be looking for ways to meet the challenge more quickly (or you could say "more easily," because that's what it will feel like to your brain).

If you apply this principle to your leadership, it's a lot easier to get everyone on board with a commitment to continual improvement. Let's say the new challenge you've set an employee has fourteen steps—so you say, "Hey, I want to make this easier for you. Can you help me figure out a way to make your job ten steps instead of fourteen?" I can guarantee you that no one will ever reply, "Gee, no thanks. I really want to keep my workload as hard as possible."

By shifting people's perspective, you empower them to start asking, "What exactly are we doing here and why?"

THE POWER OF *WHY*

I believe that one of the best ways to create a culture that's committed to continual improvement is to make a habit of asking one simple question over and over: why? In other words, why do we do it this way? As we said in Chapter 1, a business that encourages a culture of *why* has discovered the secret sauce of corporate success.

The question applies to every single aspect of your business:

Why do we do the paperwork this way?

Why do we turn in forms this way?

Why do we onboard a new employee this way?

Why do we terminate employment this way?

Why do I turn the screw fourteen times (and not thirteen or fifteen)?

Why do I set this air pressure at twenty pounds (and not fifteen or thirty)?

Why does this procedure have eight steps (and not six— or five)?

Why, why, why? I know, if you follow my advice, you'll start sounding like a two-year-old asking why the sky is blue, grass is green, and boys are different from girls. But two-year-olds' relentless curiosity is why they learn so much about the world in such a short period of time. They don't have any preconceived ideas; they're totally open to discovering new truths. As adults, we need the same attitude.

"Why?" is such a powerful question. We're not asking why over and over to cause problems. We're asking to gain a greater understanding, and because the moment we question the way we're doing things, we've opened ourselves to the possibility that there might be a better way. When we answer the question, we start to see the small details. We can suddenly pick out the steps that aren't needed. We can make whatever it is more efficient.

If you ask why and you get the answer, "Because that's the way we've always done it," you know it's time to stop and take a look at what you're doing. Chances are you need to find a new way of going about things.

> *If you have answers to the "whys," it will direct you to the "hows." As simple as that!*
> **ISRAELMORE AYIVOR**

BREAKING TRADITION

There's a great quote by Admiral Grace Hopper, who created some of the first computer programming: "The most damaging phrase in the language is 'It's always been done that way.'" It always makes me think about the woman who was cooking Thanksgiving dinner for her friends, totally confident that her turkey was going to be the most delicious they'd ever eaten because she has a secret family recipe she believes has been handed down generation after generation. What's the secret? She cuts the turkey in half and turns it upside down. She's convinced that this causes the juices to drip into the pan and evaporate, pushing steam up through the meat, making it extra juicy.

As the woman prepares the Thanksgiving meal, her mother happens to be helping her in the kitchen. When she sees her daughter cut the turkey in half and turn it upside down, she asks, "Why are you doing that?"

Her daughter is surprised, because, after all, she learned this secret from her mother. When she reminds her mother that it's the secret technique that makes the turkey moister and more delicious than any other, her mother laughs. "Honey, that's not the reason I cut the turkey in half when you were little. I cut the turkey in half because our oven was too small for the whole thing to fit."

Sometimes, when I ask why, I hear long, elaborate stories that are a lot like the daughter's turkey secret. Those stories may sound convincing at first (just like the dripping turkey juices seem to make sense), but if I keep pushing, I eventually discover that the real answer is simply "because we've always done it this way." And that's not a good enough answer.

The way we did things last year is probably not the way we should be doing them this year, and how we're doing things today won't be the way we should be doing them next year. Think about websites, for example. Five years ago, I spent hundreds of thousands of dollars having a website built that would be top of the class. And it was top of the class—five years ago. This year, when I had the website evaluated, I was told, "Your website's horrible. It doesn't do this, and it doesn't do that." We'd made the mistake of creating a website and then forgetting about it, even though the internet is the greatest marketing tool a business has in the twenty-first century. Website technology and functionality are constantly changing, which means that today's websites are a whole lot different from even the best websites created five years ago.

When it comes to your business—and to much of life—there's not much that should be set in stone. We need to be constantly adapting to a world that is always changing around us, continuously open to learning new things. So, every time you hear, "Because we've always done it that way," it's a call to attention—and it's an opportunity to utilize the kaizen principle of continual improvement.

AN ALL-PERVASIVE PRINCIPLE

A commitment to continual improvement isn't something you can apply to your professional life but not to your personal life. Look at it this way: You probably spend at least nine hours a day either being at work or thinking about work. If you sleep eight hours a night, that leaves you with seven waking hours that aren't occupied by work each day. About two hours will be spent on meals and personal hygiene stuff, leaving five hours each day that are truly yours. So, the truth is, you spend more of your life working than doing any other activity, and this means that your work values, whatever they are, will spill over into your life in general.

By the same token, who you are in your personal life will help shape who you are at work. Whenever I interview prospective employees, I always ask them two questions: "Tell me something you've learned in the last year," and "What do you do for fun?" If they can't answer the first question, and if sitting in front of the TV and cracking open a beer is their answer to the second question, then I know they aren't the right match for our organization.

People who don't have continual improvement as an all-pervasive life philosophy end up in trouble in many areas of life besides business. It happens in sports teams, in all kinds of careers, and even in marriages and friendships. If you don't keep up with the growth that's going on around you, and if you're not willing to change, eventually, one way or another, you'll have to drop out and let the others go on without you.

CHAPTER 3

LOYALTY

One of the scariest times in my business life was in 2007. I had recently gone into debt to the tune of over $8 million in order to buy out my business's other partners. Everything I owned had gone on the hook to guarantee the loan, and now I had enormous monthly payments.

My bankers and financial advisors thought I'd lost my mind. "You're a complete idiot," one of the bankers said to me in the days when I was still considering what to do. "If you go through with this deal, you're going to end up bankrupt. You might as well take everything you have, every single asset you own, throw it all out on a Las Vegas craps table—and then just hope for the best when the dice are thrown. Your odds of success are a total crapshoot."

Here's the thing, though: I knew the dice. The way I looked at it, at least four of the six sides of each die consisted of the people who made up my company. I knew the team I had, and I knew their loyalty to the company. They gave me the confidence to believe that the odds were in my favor. I was willing to take that chance.

But it was still scary. Every month I had to sweat a little (or a lot) to come up with the loan payment. When you take a loan—whether it's your first home mortgage or a student loan—at the start, the payments can seem overwhelming. After a while, though, you get used to their weight; you start taking them for granted as just one of your monthly expenses.

I wasn't at that point yet. About eight months into the loan, the payments still seemed as impossibly huge as ever. To make the pressure I was feeling even worse, the business had had a couple of slow quarters, when our revenues were down. I still believed I'd done the right thing, but I was feeling pretty stressed.

At the time, I had a little factory down in Mexico that was very important to my plan for the future. I believed that the growth I wanted my business to achieve depended on that factory, because it gave my company a pricing advantage over our competitors. That little Mexican factory was essential to my long-term sense of confidence when it came to paying off the loan. And then, early one morning, when I stumbled out of bed at 5:30 a.m., I found an e-mail waiting for me from the guy who was the plant manager at the Mexican facility. It said:

> I regret to inform you that yesterday was my last day. I
> will no longer be your plant manager in Mexico. I have
> done some terrible things, my wife is divorcing me, and
> effective immediately, I will no longer be working with
> you.

My heart felt as though it had, literally, dropped like a stone, all the way down to my feet. Hank had been with me eleven years. He had started out as a press-brake operator, bending metal, and then he'd come up through the ranks, the same way I had. He knew the ins and outs of the processes, and I trusted him absolutely.

With him suddenly off the job, I had visions of three hundred employees walking out the door, taking with them anything that wasn't nailed down. I could lose millions of dollars of equipment, and if that happened, my entire business was going to go under. I thought, *Man, that banker was right—I rolled the dice and I just crapped out.*

I grabbed my phone and tried calling Hank. No answer. "No, no, no, no!" I said to myself as I wrote him an e-mail—and then I wrote the same words:

No, no, no, no. If you need to give notice, that's fine, but not like this. You can't do this to me.

I don't panic very easily, but at that moment I was definitely panicked. I was barely out of bed, but I threw on some clothes—no time for a shower!—jumped in my car, and set off on the two-and-a-half-hour drive down to the factory. I was on the phone the whole time, trying to get ahold of people. If I couldn't reach Hank, then I needed to at least do damage control.

Finally, I reached the HR manager in Mexico, Iliana Rivera, the future plant manager.

"Hey," I said, trying to sound casual. I knew I needed to keep the panic out of my voice. "Hank isn't going to be in today. If he sent any e-mails to anybody else, disregard them." For all I knew, the guy had e-mailed the entire company. Everyone could be as panicked as I was. I needed to get control of the situation, but since I didn't know what he had done, I was groping in the dark.

By the time I arrived at the factory, it was about an hour into its first shift. I called Iliana to come down, and I gathered all the department leaders together. These were young managers without a lot of experience, and they were devastated when they heard that Hank had resigned.

The factory had something going for it, though—a culture that gave it strength in a way that few American businesses have. Mexican workers' social lives revolve around their work relationships. The Mexican team celebrates their daughters' quinceañeras together. If someone's mom dies, everyone contributes something to help pay for the funeral. There's a sense of camaraderie, a feeling that everyone is family, more so than I've ever seen between workers in the United States.

So now, their unity helped make them a strong team, but it also meant that they took Hank's resignation personally. They felt betrayed. "You mean he just abandoned us?" they asked.

I nodded. By this time, I'd forced myself to accept the truth and get past my own feelings of disbelief and betrayal. "Yeah," I said, "he's not coming back."

I was working hard to sound matter-of-fact and businesslike. I didn't want them to hear despair in my voice, but as I looked around at the people gathered in the room, my heart sank even lower. There was not a single person there, I believed, who had the experience or the ability to manage the three hundred people in that facility. By this time, my heart was just lying there on the floor.

The only conclusion I could reach was that I would have to do it. I sucked in a long breath and squared my shoulders. *That's it*, I thought. *I'm the guy with the most experience in manufacturing in the company. I'm going to have to be the guy that does it. I don't know how I'll do it, but I'll have to be the president of the company, the owner of the company, and at the same time, I'll have to be down here in Mexico to be the plant manager.*

I wasn't quite ready to commit to it out loud, though, and since there wasn't anything more I could say, I dismissed them all. One guy, however, hung back after the others had left. "Hey," he said, "can I talk to you about this?"

Angel had worked with our US facility for quite a while, and now he was in Mexico to train the painters there. He had gone through workshops in lean management, and he was a good departmental manager, but right then I really didn't feel like talking to him. "Not right now, Angel," I said. "I just can't talk right now."

I didn't want to be rude, but I was hanging on by a thread, so I pushed him out of the room and shut the door. Then I sank into a chair, trying to think of options. I wondered if there were anyone who could do this besides me. Whom did I know? Whom could I call? Whom did I trust? I needed somebody who could do more than just manage the numbers. I needed somebody who would love the people, who would be loyal to them, who would make decisions based on all our long-term philosophies.

I always say my managers need to add value to the organization by developing our people. They have to keep mentoring and coaching them. This isn't an outlook or a skill that's easy to find. My head dropped into my hands. Who would I get?

I couldn't sit there, doing nothing, so I started making phone calls. One of the calls was to a headhunter. When she heard I needed somebody the same day—right then, not in a month or two—she didn't offer me much hope. None of my other calls got me anywhere either, and I was back to the only option I'd been able to come up with from the start: I would have to do it myself.

Finally, I pulled myself together, got up, and left the room where I'd been sitting for what seemed like hours. When I went out into the hall, there was Angel, my paint trainer. All that time, he'd been patiently waiting for me to come out.

"What's up?" I asked him.

"Can I talk to you, boss?"

"Sure," I said. There was nothing else I could do right then, so I figured I might as well find out what he wanted. "What's going on?"

"Well," Angel said, "I was wondering—what are you going to do?"

I told him the truth. "I don't know."

He came up with the name of someone who might be able to manage the plant, but I said, "No, she can't do it. She has this family issue she's dealing with. She wouldn't be able to handle more responsibility right now."

Then he suggested the name of someone else, but this time I had to point out that the individual lacked a couple of essential skills for the job.

And then Angel said, "Well, boss, you know you can count on me."

I stared at him for a moment. I'd never even considered asking Angel to do the job, because he didn't live in Mexico. He was only in Mexico temporarily, to lead a training program. His home was 160 miles away, out by our US facility. But as I looked at him, I felt a flicker of hope—and my heart lifted just a tiny bit.

"Angel," I said slowly, "do you think you could just . . . just kind of take care of people for a little bit? Make sure that the factory runs according to plan and that we build a good product—just until I can figure out something else?"

"Sure," he said, and the way he met my eyes gave my heart an even greater boost. "I'm here for the company, and I'm here for you. Whatever you need, I'll do it."

"But where would you stay?"

"Don't worry about that. That's not your concern. I'll work it out if you need me to be here." He gave me a smile. "So do you need me here, boss?"

I gave a big sigh of relief. "I need you to be here, Angel."

What had started out as a temporary solution turned into a long-term position for Angel. For the next five years, Angel was the plant manager in Mexico. He never asked me for a raise. He never asked me for a housing allowance. He just was there, doing the job, because that's what the company needed.

Of course, I did compensate him, eventually, but those next few months were chaotic. I had a lot on my mind, and I'm embarrassed to say I forgot. He never said a word to me, and he did an incredible job. Then, at the midyear review, as I was looking over payroll files, I realized what I'd done. I picked up the phone immediately.

"Hey, I am so sorry," I told him.

"I wasn't worried about it. I knew sooner or later you'd see it."

"Are you mad?" I asked him. I wouldn't have blamed him at all if he had been.

"What am I going to be mad about?" he asked me. "This company has always been good to me, Aaron. I trust you. I wasn't worried in the least."

A few years after that, the Mexican plant was still going strong. In fact, it was growing, and the number of employees had tripled to nine hundred. Angel was having a few health issues, and he decided it was time for him to move on to the next thing in his life. He'd still be working for me, but in a different position. Iliana, the HR manager, became the next plant manager, and Angel stayed on long enough to mentor her for another two years. A woman plant manager is pretty rare in Mexico, but Iliana did a fantastic job, thanks in part to Angel.

A few years later, I ran into an issue at our facility in China. I went over there and spent two weeks trying to deal with it, and then I sent somebody else over there for another two weeks, but it still wasn't solved. As we discussed the problem at a manager meeting, somebody said, "It's not going to be solved until we inject our DNA into the facility there for longer than a week or two. We need somebody to go over there who's at a higher level."

I knew she was right, but I didn't know how to make it happen. I looked around the room at my managers, wondering who I was going to send to China for four or five months.

And then I saw a hand go up—and once again, it was Angel's hand. "I can go to China," he said.

I shook my head. "No, you can't. Your wife needs you at home." I knew she'd been having health issues, and I don't ever want my employees to think their families have to come second to their jobs.

"She's better now," Angel said. "She's fine, in fact."

I still hesitated.

"Does the company need me to go, boss?"

And there it was again, almost the same question he'd asked me before. Once again, he didn't ask, "How much will you pay me if I'll do this job for you?" Instead, he asked, "Do you need me?"

I looked at him and nodded. "We need you to go."

"Alright then," he said. "I'll go."

He took a flight to China the next day, and he spent months there, injecting our DNA into our facility by coaching, mentoring, and teaching. Once again, his loyalty saved the day.

That was a few years ago. Since then Angel has been living in Mexico, acting as an advisor to the current plant manager. He now has years of wisdom and experience to share, so I think of him as an old sensei (teacher or master). Recently, though, in the middle of a big meeting, he suddenly vomited blood.

His fellow workers down there—who by this time knew and loved the guy like a member of the family—tried to persuade him to go to the hospital, but Angel wanted to finish the meeting first.

"If you don't go to the hospital right now," one of them told him, "I'm calling Aaron."

That was enough to persuade him to go, but he was still thinking he'd be able to finish the meeting later that day. The doctor who examined him said, "You're not going anywhere. Your appendix burst, and you need immediate surgery."

Today my company is so big that I don't know everything that happens from day to day, so I didn't learn what had happened to Angel until several weeks later. By that time, Angel was back home, but he still wasn't able to work, and my controller had put him on disability.

Disability insurance doesn't pay full wages. In fact, it only pays a small fraction of them, and it's pretty much impossible to live on it. When I heard what had happened, I was furious. I stormed into our Las Vegas office and told my CFO, my controller, and the president of the company, "I will fire all three of you right here, right now."

Later, folks told me they'd never seen me so angry, but you do not put a guy on disability who has always been there for the company, someone who has stood up and said, "Here I am. I'll be accountable for this situation. I'll take responsibility."

"If you do not show loyalty to our people," I shouted at my executives, "I don't care what your position is. I don't care who you are. Your employment can be terminated today, because if you're not loyal to our greatest asset—our people—I will not be loyal to you."

My CFO stepped up to the plate and said, "It was my mistake. We should have never, ever have done that."

"Darn right," I muttered, still too angry to do anything but charge out of the room to call Angel.

I couldn't get hold of him. Once again, for the second time in my career, I was truly starting to panic, but this time it wasn't because of money; it was because I knew we had let someone down. I called some other people to find out if they knew where Angel was, and I finally reached him.

"Qué pasa, jefe?" he said, and I could hear he was laughing. As so often happens in organizations, the grapevine had reached him faster than I had. "I hear you're on fire right now."

"I am so sorry, my friend," I said. "I am so ashamed that we let you down like this, after everything you have done for us. Everything you have done for me."

"It's okay, boss. I wasn't too worried. I knew that when you found out, everything would be okay."

We talked a little longer, and then, when I got off the phone, I sent him this e-mail:

Angel, as you know, one of our core values is loyalty. You have shown great loyalty to the company and to me, and we will show you the same. There is no need for you to take disability pay while you're unable to work. We will pay you your full salary as you recover. I want you fully healed before you return, my friend. Please be assured that the company is very grateful for all the many years of service and hard work you've given. I hope and pray for a speedy recovery. Please rest stress-free, knowing that all is well. See you soon, my friend.

LOYALTY CREATES GREAT COMPANIES

Want to build an amazing company? Be loyal to your people. By yourself, you'll never be able to build something amazing. There is absolutely no way a single individual will ever build a great organization. A great organization is built by the minds and the hearts of many people—and what pulls them all together is loyalty: your loyalty to them, and theirs to you and to each other. You have to defend the loyalty of the company with all of your heart.

What does loyalty mean when it comes to a business? *Merriam Webster's Dictionary* defines loyalty as "showing complete and constant support for someone or something." I believe that's a two-way relationship. I can't expect my employees to be loyal to me and the company if I'm not loyal to them. They have to be completely confident that they have my total and constant support before I can have theirs.

As I struggled to put all this into words for my son, trying to explain to him why he'll need loyalty if he wants to step into my shoes one day, I finally came up with this: "First and foremost, business is about people. **More than anything else—more than customers or shareholders even—a business's success depends on the people who work there.** You can't create a good product without those people, you won't build customer loyalty without them, and you won't earn profits for your shareholders without them. Business owners who forget that—who start thinking that their workers are an expendable, replaceable resource—will inevitably end up with a weak business that won't survive."

Recently, I spoke with two business owners who weren't convinced that their workers were essential to their business's success. I asked them, "What is the product that your franchisees are selling?"

"We're selling the service of hospice care in a person's own home," they answered.

"And how does that service get delivered?"

They looked a little uncomfortable, because they were starting to see where I was headed. "By our caregivers."

"Exactly," I said. "The service you're delivering is one human being going to another human being's home at a really tough time in life and providing some dignity and comfort in that individual's last days." I waited for a moment to see if they understood what I was saying, and then I added, "Everything in your business is about your caregivers. Every decision you make needs to be about your caregivers. Otherwise, you don't even have a service to sell."

In my business, I'm selling a product instead of a service, but that product doesn't make itself. I've toured thousands of manufacturing facilities around the world, and I've yet to see a factory that was 100 percent automated. Total automation is cost prohibitive unless you're producing something that's consumed by the millions every day (aluminum cans, for example). Take a car factory: A really busy manufacturing facility might build three hundred cars a day. You can automate some of the steps, but if you were to build a machine to install three hundred gas caps a day, you'd never get your money back. Hiring human beings to do that job makes more sense in terms of cost.

Any business depends on people to deliver goods and services. Those people are the most important asset any business has. They're more important than machinery, more important than plant facilities, more important than intellectual property. So doesn't it make sense to cultivate and protect that asset?

> *Employee loyalty begins with employer loyalty.*
> **HARVEY MACKAY**

PROTECTING YOUR ASSETS

When people like those two health-care franchisors push back on this statement, they usually say something along the lines of, "Oh, come on. That's just feel-good bull crap. I'm not a social worker." Well, no, as business leaders we're not social workers. But forget any moral or philosophical issues, and, for a second, think of employees as though they were any other kind of asset.

Let's say your business owns a private jet. That jet cost the company about $10 million. So are you going to leave it outside 365 days a year to be rained on, to be baked in the heat, to be frozen in the cold? Well, if you do, your $10 million jet won't last very long. So you either buy or rent a hangar, which can end up being 10 or 20 percent of the original cost of the jet, and you put your jet inside the hangar to protect it. You wax the jet, you wash it, you clean it, and you maintain it. You have a mechanic—who is also very expensive—come once a month to do maintenance. Once a year, he does a thorough maintenance overhaul of the entire aircraft.

The thing about owning jets is that you have to not only think about the cost of the jet up front but also the cost of ownership. That's what stops many people from getting a jet. It's not buying the jet that's so terribly expensive; it's owning it. The cost of upkeep on this particular asset is tremendous, and yet any business that has decided to purchase a private jet doesn't think twice about investing in the jet's ongoing upkeep.

When it comes to human beings, though, I've encountered business owners who, figuratively speaking, leave their people to be soaked in the rain, baked in the sun, and frozen in winter storms. They act as though their human assets are dispensable and easily replaced.

No doubt about it, as a business owner you can fire and hire new people all the time. With the unemployment numbers the way they are these days, you'll always be able to find someone who's looking for work. Yet, anybody who is even a little bit smart in business will tell you that a constant turnover of workers is expensive. It slows productivity, and it costs you money in terms of training. In fact, it's probably the single biggest, most expensive waste a business has. Additionally, a revolving door is horrible for morale. Would you feel safe working at a place where people are constantly getting fired or quitting? So, when you look at it that way, even if you have the coldest, most selfish heart in the world, you'll still want to build loyalty into your business.

> *Employees are a company's greatest asset—they're your competitive advantage. You want to attract and retain the best; provide them with encouragement, stimulus, and make them feel that they are an integral part of the company's mission.*
> **ANNE M. MULCAHY**

BUILDING LOYALTY

The kind of loyalty Angel demonstrated doesn't get built overnight. The foundation is a long history of you, as the business leader, making the right choices, even sometimes at your own expense, for the well-being of the people who make up your company. If you were to have a goose that laid golden eggs, to what extreme would you go to protect it, care for it, and make sure it did what you needed it to do—lay golden eggs? *You would go to any length.* The people in your organization are as valuable as that goose! Management decisions need to be based on long-term philosophies that focus on building and growing the business's people, even at the expense of short-term financial goals. Loyalty has to start with you, the leader. You must have a deep commitment: "First and foremost, I'm going to make sure my people are taken care of."

I'm not saying it's always easy to make people your priority. In fact, it may mean that, once in a while, you go without pay to make sure your employees get *their* paychecks (if you are a business owner). My philosophy has always been that since I stand to reap the most benefit from my business's success, I should also be the one who suffers the most pain. I have to accept both sides of the equation.

Sometimes, you may need to go to your workers and say something along these lines: "Here's the situation. Right now we have a shortfall of $100,000 a month. We're not making enough to cover our costs, and we have to fill the gap. We can fire X number of people to make it up—or we can cut everybody's pay by 5 percent. We have to do one or the other or we're going to bleed to death—and then all of us will be out of work."

That's the way I've always tried to handle these situations. The answers aren't easy for anyone. Sometimes, people take a pay reduction, and then positions still need to be cut in order to make the business leaner and more efficient. No one's ever happy about making less money, and no one wants to be responsible for people losing their jobs. But my loyalty to them means they trust me to tell them what's really going on. I give them the power to be part of any decision that's made. I don't just walk in one day and announce, "I'm cutting everyone's pay—and then I'm doing away with thirty positions."

If there's a problem, it's not just the leader's problem; it's everyone's. And what's even better is that it's not up to you, as the leader, to find the solution by yourself. You have an entire team of very smart people who may come up with answers that never occurred to you.

Once, when my business was in a financial crunch and I presented the problem to my employees, one of them said, "Hey, we have room on the day shift. Why don't we shut down the second shift? It would cut our electric bill in half, and then we'd be able to keep jobs." It had never occurred me to look at ways to spend less electricity. As it turned out, cutting out the shift got us well on our way to our financial goal—and helped us maintain jobs in the process.

LOYALTY ISN'T A CRAPSHOOT

If I could sit down today with those same bankers who advised me so strongly not to bet everything I had on my business, here's what I'd say to them: "This isn't rocket science, and it isn't feel-good sentiment. It's common sense. When I invest my loyalty in my employees, I earn their loyalty in return, and that leads to success. It's an equation with a consistent and predictable result. Add "A" plus "B," and you don't get a whole multitude of unpredictable things. No, you get C every time. There's no chance involved. Oh, there may be a few variables involved I can't control. But I'm not throwing any dice, and it isn't a crapshoot. I'm pretty confident about how things will turn out."

Invest in employees—be loyal to them—and your business will be a success. It's as simple as that.

In her book *The Loyalty Advantage,* Dianne M. Durkin describes the practical necessity of loyalty:

Our earliest ancestors probably learned that loyalty was a valuable survival tool. In the jungle, the desert, or the open plains, *loyalty* to your tribe increased your chances of surviving harsh weather and an unreliable supply of food and water.

Durkin has also said, "Employees are the most valuable asset of a company and need to be valued and validated through programs and processes that help them grow both personally and professionally."

CHAPTER 4
ENJOY HARD WORK

Recently, when my son and I were in the car together, he said to me, "I hate homework."

"How come?" I asked him.

"I just don't like it," he said.

"What don't you like?"

"It's boring."

"Boring?" I turned my head to give him a look. "Do you think everything in life is going to be fun?"

"Well, no, not fun," he said, "but it doesn't have to be boring."

"You're right," I told him. "It doesn't have to be boring. But that's up to you. Boring is a choice."

I'm not sure if he understood what I was telling him, but it's a fact: boring isn't like something being cold or hot, salty or sweet. Instead, it's a decision we make. It's something we tell ourselves about certain activities or work. We could choose to tell ourselves something different.

And we might as well, because there's no way around it: The daily grind of hard work is the key to success, so we might as well learn to execute it with pleasure.

FIND YOUR MOTIVATION

I will have lunch or talk to any CEO or entrepreneur who wants to talk. I meet them through YPO, CEO forums, in the community, workshops I attend, and even a few from my barber! I have never charged a single penny, nor would I. I have deep empathy for what they are trying to achieve and the knowledge I have gained I am happy to share for free. I will meet with them quarterly as long as I see them doing the work that we have talked about and making progress.

When young entrepreneurs ask me for advice about getting a start-up going, one of the first questions I always ask is, "Why are you doing this?"

As you might guess, a common answer is, "I want to make a ton of money. I think this is a million-dollar idea."

So then I say, "What's your endgame? What do you ultimately want to achieve?"

Many times, they give me an answer I really hate to hear, something along the lines of, "I'm going to build this to the point where I can get private equity funding or venture capital funding, and then I'm going to sell it for twenty times the amount of money I put into it."

"So that's your goal?" I ask them.

And they say, "That's my goal."

Then I tell them something they don't want to hear: "I wouldn't do it."

"What do you mean?" they say. "It's a great idea."

"I didn't say it wasn't a great idea," I say. "But the reason you gave me—because of all the money you're going to make—well, I would not do it for that reason. It won't be enough to make you work as hard as you'll have to if you want your business to succeed. It won't be enough to get you out of bed in the morning on a rainy day."

I've learned that if you're only in it for the money, when those gray, rainy days come (and I promise they will), you're going to say, "I don't want to get up and face my work all over again." And sooner or later, you're going to walk away, because the only way you can enjoy hard work is by having a goal that's bigger than money. On those days when your job looks like just a bunch of mindless, tedious work, you need to know *why* you're doing the work; you need to be able to say, "By doing this, I'm going to achieve something amazing. I'm going to change the world." You need to be motivated by something greater than money.

I've found this principle applies to most aspects of life. For example, I keep myself in pretty good shape. I don't have a lot of time in my life, but I make a point of getting in a thirty-minute workout most days. I also keep myself on my routine when it comes to what I eat. I wake up every morning and drink a protein shake. I make it myself: a scoop and a half of protein, a handful of frozen berries, and water.

People say to me, sometimes, "You eat that *every* morning? Don't you get bored with it? Don't you want bacon and eggs some mornings?

But it's all about my mind-set. I'm not telling myself, "Oh gosh, I have to drink this same boring thing again this morning." Instead,

I genuinely think those shakes are delicious. Even more important, I know those shakes get my day off to a good start. They help me be ready to take on the world. And that's a powerful motivation.

I wasn't always like this. Back in my early thirties, I'd be working ninety hours a week and eating fast food on the go. I'd be up at five in the morning and out the door twenty minutes later. On the way to work, at the Jack in the Box drive through, I'd get two grilled sourdough breakfast sandwiches, which I'd have eaten by the time I reached the office. And then I'd struggle through my day. It's hard to work hard when you have no energy!

I like to have energy, and I need a whole lot of it to do the work I do. So, I was motivated to change the way I eat, and I continue to be motivated to keep my healthy routine. I like the feeling it gives me that I can take on the world. I have learned to find joy in exercise and a healthy diet, things that many Americans struggle with. I don't eat a lot of starchy foods. I don't eat much junk food. To be honest, it's not even particularly hard for me. I don't feel I have to use incredible willpower to deny myself, because my ultimate goal is completely selfish: I want to feel good. I know if I eat junk food, it will, ultimately, make me feel unwell. Knowing that makes healthy food taste delicious. It really does.

Enjoying hard work in business takes the same kind of motivation. We talked about the *why* being important to your corporate culture, but it's equally important to you and your employees' ability to enjoy hard work. When something inspires you, you're willing to work hard for it. You know *why* you're working so hard, and that gives you joy.

> *People who love going to work are more productive and more creative. They go home happier and have happier families. They treat their colleagues and clients and customers better. Inspired employees make for stronger companies and stronger economies.*
> **SIMON SINEK**

Recently, my son had to write a book report as a homework assignment. He's a good reader (far better than I was at his age), but he really didn't want to write the book report. "It's *boring*," he said. "I don't know why we can't just read books. Why do we have to write stupid reports about them?"

"Tell me about the book you read," I told him.

"Well, it was about the *Hindenburg*," he said.

"So tell me about the *Hindenburg*," I said. "How did it work? What happened?"

He really couldn't answer my questions, so I looked at his book report assignment. We worked though the questions, reading the book as we went. When we were all done, I said, "See, Jack, the purpose of book reports is to teach you to understand and remember what you read."

I don't know if my son really understood what I was saying. I know he'll have more book reports in the future, so I guess I'll find out then. I'm just hoping I'll be able to find ways to teach him the secret of enjoying hard work the way my dad taught me.

FIND THE TREASURE

If there's one thing my dad knew how to teach, it was how to work hard. He'd done it his entire life. He started out with a paper route when he was just a kid, and then, as a teenager, he went to work in a dairy. After that, he worked for an insurance company, doing the only career a guy without a college degree could do and make money: He was a salesman. He loved people, and he loved talking to them, so I think that was what really motivated him.

And my dad worked hard, really hard. Monday through Friday, he was always gone when I woke up. When I went to bed at eight o'clock, he'd still be at work. I pretty much only saw him on the weekends. So, on weekends, he took advantage of his time to teach me the things that were important to him.

That didn't mean we threw balls in the backyard! No, every Saturday my dad would get up and say to me, "Okay. Go get your work clothes on. We're going to go out in the backyard and do yard work."

My sister and I would exchange looks, but we'd do what he said. Our family had a half-acre lot, which in Southern California is considered a big piece of land. It had a front lawn that needed to be mowed and edged, and it had flower beds that needed to be weeded. Worst of all, in the backyard, was a woodpile. That's the place where I really learned my dad's lesson about hard work.

Our house had a fireplace where we burned real logs. We didn't need a fire for warmth, of course (not in Southern California), but my dad loved the way a fire smelled and looked. He didn't want to spend money on firewood, though, so whenever anyone had a tree that had fallen, we'd take my dad's old Ford pickup to get the wood. Then it was my job to unload the truck and stack the wood up against the cinder-block walls that enclosed our backyard.

That woodpile grew to be about six feet tall and probably close to ninety feet long, and my job, two or three Saturdays a month, was to clean the woodpile. This involved raking all the leaves away from the pile. It also meant picking up any poop that had accumulated during the week from our dogs. Most of all, cleaning the woodpile meant picking up avocados.

To this day, I have never seen an avocado tree as big as the one in our backyard. The diameter of its trunk was around two and a half feet, and it had to have been seventy or eighty years old. It was an enormous tree, and it dropped a massive amount of fruit into our backyard. The avocados were great to eat—we even took them around to neighbors and sold them—but the problem with avocado trees in Southern California is that they attract fruit rats. If you don't pick the fruit up as it falls on the ground, you'll end up with rats in your yard.

So, that's why my sister and I had to clean the woodpile. We raked up everything that had accumulated on the ground over the week—leaves, rotten avocados, dog poop—and made an enormous pile, probably five or six feet across. Then we had to scoop it up in our hands and throw it in the trashcan. This was the part we *really* hated. We'd try to find ways to get around it—but my dad would say, "There's nothing wrong with getting your hands dirty."

I dreaded Saturday mornings. When we were younger, my sister and I would cry and complain to our mom, "Dad's being so mean to us!" But that didn't get us out of the work. Sometimes, I'd get a splinter in my hand from the wood, and I'd go running back inside for my mom to take a look at it. My dad would look up from whatever he was doing and say, "When you're done with that, get back outside. You've got to finish that woodpile today." I hated it!

Then one Saturday, when I took a break from the woodpile, I walked in the house and found my dad in his recliner, drinking a Dr. Pepper and eating popcorn. I looked at him and said, "*You're* not working. So how come I have to? I'm out there busting my butt, and you're just sitting in here doing nothing." Keep in mind I was only nine years old; it's my only excuse!

My mom, who very seldom raised her voice, yelled at me, "Don't you dare say that to your father. You don't have any idea how hard he works all week."

Meanwhile, my father had gotten out of his recliner and was coming toward me.

I'm dead, I thought. *He's going to kill me.*

He didn't say anything, just grabbed my arm and pulled me out to the backyard. He pointed at the woodpile. "Do you understand why I tell you to do this every Saturday?"

When I shook my head, he said, "I want you to get all this wood off the ground so the rats don't get into it. So, you're going to need to stack some cinder blocks to raise the woodpile off the ground, and then you're going to have to move all the wood from where it is now onto the cinder blocks."

I believed his story about getting the wood off the ground because of the rats, though I know now he was feeding me a line. But, I still didn't want to move that entire pile of wood and then restack it all on the cinder blocks.

"Uh-uh," I said.

He gave me a stern look. "You need to do it."

"But I don't want to," I whined. "It's boring."

He looked me in the eye and said, "Do you think life is nothing but fun, Son?"

"Yeah," I said. "It's mostly fun, but this is boring. I don't want to do it. The wood's fine right here."

I remember he just looked at me for a moment and then said, "Listen to me, Son. Life is hard, so you have two choices. You can decide to let life be hard for you forever and be a whiner and complainer. Or, you can decide to take control of life and enjoy doing the things that are hard."

Well, when you're nine years old, you want to go ride your bike. You don't want to enjoy hard work.

"Move the woodpile, Son," my dad said, "because this is a battle you're not going to win. So you might as well get busy."

I moved the woodpile. It took me a couple of Saturdays to finish the job—and then, two or three weeks later, he asked me to move it again. It became a regular thing. And you know what happened? I started to kind of enjoy it. I found things in the wood, little treasures—an old tool, a nest of baby rats—and the work started to seem like a treasure hunt to me. I started looking forward to whatever I would find this time.

As I got a little older, I asked myself, "What else can I do to make this job more fun?" Well, I'm not a particularly artistic person, but I started making designs and patterns with the logs. The work went faster now. I'm not saying it only *seemed* to go faster, though it did. It actually did go faster. Instead of having to work all day Saturday, the way I always had before, I'd be done by eleven o'clock or noon. I'd have time to go do other things.

When I was sixteen, I started getting jobs. People always commented on what a hard worker I was—and I knew whom I had to thank for that.

One of the best compliments my father ever paid me was when he said to me, "Son, I don't know anybody who works harder than you." Thanks to my dad and that woodpile, I not only knew how to work hard, but I also found a way to enjoy every job I ever had.

THE MAGIC INGREDIENT

Why are some people successful and others not? I believe that enjoying hard work is the magic ingredient. It can make you or break you. Obviously, not everyone who works hard is going to become a millionaire. But, I can guarantee you'll never starve to death. As my dad liked to say, "The world always needs a hard worker."

There's a reason why work is different from a vacation. Work isn't meant to be easy; it's meant to challenge us. We need vacations every now and then, but we also need challenges. They are what make life interesting. The president of my company, Steve Hoffa, says all the time, "Business is nothing more than a set of problems we have to solve." That's what our work is: There's a problem. Let's find a solution . . . Here's a new problem. Let's find a solution. You could replace the word *problem* with *opportunity*. However we may think of business issues, we're constantly solving things. In the process, we learn and grow.

When you start looking at hard work that way—as the path to becoming a better person every single day—I guarantee you'll start enjoying your work. Instead of thinking, *This is so boring*, you'll think, *What can I learn today? What treasure will I discover in the woodpile?* That's the magic ingredient that turns the daily grind into the exhilaration of mountain climbing.

Climbing a mountain is hard work, but reaching the top feels pretty awesome. The view is amazing.

And as you look out from your new vantage point, you'll see there are even taller mountains out there. There are more challenges, more hard work—and more ways to grow. So, enjoy the view. Then start climbing again.

When I'm talking to MBA students, I often tell them, "If you want to be successful, drop out of your MBA for a little bit. Go get a job in construction. Go get a job in plumbing. Go get a job on a manufacturing plant floor in an entry-level position. Then learn to find joy doing the tasks they're going to give you."

They look at me as if I were crazy, of course, but then I say, "By doing hard manual work, you'll get the strength you're going to need to grind out those long, long days that lie ahead, if you want to be a leader in business.

You'll learn that hard work doesn't kill you and that, in fact, you can even learn to enjoy it. Because, if you can't learn that, if you're going to cut and run the first time work seems arduous or tedious, then you don't have what it takes to be a business leader."

When you're a business leader, you're responsible for people's lives—their first homes, their kids' college educations, their retirement savings, and their ability to give to charities and help take care of the poor and hungry. If you can't take the hard work that will be required of you, you don't have the right to ask all these folks to put their trust in you.

> *Winners embrace hard work. They love the discipline of it, the trade-off they're making to win. Losers, on the other hand, see it as punishment. And that's the difference.*
> **LOU HOLTZ**

My dad gave me a plaque with a quotation from Ella Wheeler Wilcox that I hung in my office: **"There is no chance, no fate, no destiny that can circumvent or hinder or control the firm resolve of a determined soul."** Enjoying hard work is very much an act of determination. It's being determined to grind it out and come to the end that's expected or desired. It's based on understanding the *why* of what we're doing, not just the *how*. And, when we commit to enjoying our work, no matter how hard it is, we continually improve.

CHAPTER 5
ACTIONS SPEAK LOUDER THAN WORDS

When you see a male lion's face, what do you think of? Courage? Nobility? Pride? Strength? Human beings have associated all these qualities with male lions for thousands of years. Anthropologists tell us that the image of a maned lion is one of the most ancient and most recognizable of all human symbols. So what did the lion do to earn his reputation?

An older male lion is the leader of his pride—but the job description is pretty simple. He lies around all day while the lionesses and younger males go out and do the hunting. When the kill is brought back to the pride, he gets to eat first. He mates multiple times a day, he eats, he sleeps. That's about it.

Except that every once in a while, he opens his mouth and roars. That roar calls the members of his pride, while at the same time it tells invaders to "Get out! Or you'll be sorry."

We've all heard the MGM lion roar, but that's nothing like the experience of hearing an actual lion roar. The first time I heard it, I was on a safari in Tanzania. Darkness had just fallen, and I was settling into my tent when a terrible sound filled up every bit of air around me. It felt as though the beast were just outside my tent. A roar like that can travel miles. The lion's diaphragm is enormous, and he uses it to produce an immense, bone-shaking noise that tells every hyena, wild dog, and leopard for miles around to run.

If the lion's roar weren't followed up by action, however, I doubt he'd have become the symbol of strength and authority that he has. For millennia, his actions have spoken even louder than his roar. He doesn't let out a roar just because he's bored and doesn't have anything better to do. He's not roaring for the heck of it. He roars because he means business. He's warning every animal within sound of his voice. They know if they don't get out of there, they'll have to fight the lion—or be eaten.

> *Talk doesn't cook rice.*
> **CHINESE PROVERB**

PUT YOUR MONEY WHERE YOUR MOUTH IS

As human beings, we might say we too have prides, groups that are led by powerful leaders. But unfortunately, our leaders often roar, roar, roar and never follow up with action. In other words, they don't put their money where their mouth is.

I know, I know. You've heard this a million times before. It's not as if I'm expressing some revolutionary idea. But, the thing is, much of the time, we don't let our actions speak louder than our words. I'm as guilty of that as the next person. As leaders, we give lip service to a lot of great ideas. We've read all the books, and we know the lingo. But our actions don't line up with our talk. We do a lot of roaring, but people don't pay much attention, because they have learned that it's just noise.

Any time we stand up to announce a policy change or implement a new procedure, we should stop first and reflect on two important questions.

- *Am I willing to do whatever it is myself?* I've learned the answer to that question needs to be the litmus test I give myself before I open my mouth. I shouldn't be asking people to do things that I'm unwilling to do myself.

- *Am I already doing this?* In other words, have I tested this before asking that my staff deploy a new policy or process? Have I tried it out? As leaders, before we ask our staff to go in a different direction, we need to use the scientific method (testing, observing, measuring). In my company, we call it PDCA: plan, do, check, act. Before initiating anything that puts new demands on our staff, we need to identify the root causes of the problem, the things we are going to change to address the problem, how we will measure success or failure, and what we will adjust if needed. This is a way of thinking, but it's also a process that creates action, the sort of action that speaks far louder than any words we could ever say.

> *Remember, people will judge you by your actions,*
> *not your intentions. You may have a heart of gold—*
> *but so does a hard-boiled egg.*
> **AUTHOR UNKNOWN**

A CULTURE OF DOERS, NOT TALKERS

If you create a corporate culture that doesn't tolerate failure, you'll also have culture where action is more important than talk. My company is a hard-charging organization, constantly trying to take new territory. We're not competitive in the sense that we're looking to prove ourselves better than anyone else. We simply like to succeed at whatever we put our hand to. We look for challenges—and then we overcome them. This requires that we constantly examine ourselves. We ask ourselves over and over, "What's not working? And how do we fix it?"

Creating this kind of confident, action-oriented culture doesn't mean, however, that you try to implement a million different things, a new flavor of the week at every staff meeting. Instead, it requires a level of focus that keeps you from running in too many directions at once. Otherwise, your meetings will become just talk, talk, talk— and instead of charging up the next hill, you'll end up off in the weeds somewhere, stuck in a ditch going nowhere.

At my company, we have a tool box full of things I've found very useful for keeping meetings on task: stuffed animals. A couple that get pulled out fairly often are the kitty cat and the lion. When these furry creatures get tossed at you, you know you're being reminded that you are either roaring like a lion or meowing like a kitty cat. Are your words backed up by power? Another stuffed animal we throw at folks to keep them focused is the parrot. Parrots sit in their cages and talk, talk, talk, but they don't actually do much of anything. If someone on my staff finds herself holding the parrot, she knows she's been pontificating too long. We're not there to talk; we're there to determine the best action to take next.

> *Action is eloquence.*
> **WILLIAM SHAKESPEARE**

THE POWER OF ACTION

When I think back on my career, the employees who have been the most valuable to me—those go-to people, the ones I knew I could count on—were always the quiet ones. They didn't talk a lot about what they were going to do; they just did it. They were the ones who didn't need to sit around talking about a problem. Instead, they said, "Cut to the chase. What do we need to do?"

Many years ago, I was trying to find a way for management to help the manufacturing workers make more money. Working with steel is hot, hard work, and the workers were doing it in a dark, old building that was far from an ideal work environment. I decided that if they got paid on a per-piece basis, they would be able to make more money while, at the same time, production would increase.

So, I called the workers together, and I said, "Today we're going to change the way you get paid. From now on, you're going to keep a tally of every single piece you complete each day. We'll assign a value to those pieces, and your pay will be based on how much work you complete." I was genuinely trying to help these guys. I thought the new pay structure would motivate them to work harder, while allowing them to make more money.

This was early in my career, though, and I hadn't yet learned that people panic when anything changes the way they are paid. As soon as I closed my mouth, hands were shooting up all over the room, and I was peppered with questions. About 20 percent of the guys there said they were quitting.

And now I was starting to panic, because I knew if 20 percent of the workers walked off the job, I was in trouble. I did my best to explain why I was making the change and how it could help them, but the grumbling was drowning me out.

Suddenly, though, we heard the sound of a grinder starting up. We all fell silent, listening to the *rrrrippp-rrrippp* of the metal. I took a deep breath and told the room, "Look, everyone, just go to lunch and calm down. Nobody quit, and we'll talk about it after lunch, okay?"

Then, when everyone else had left, I walked over to the worker who had started up the grinder. "What are you doing, Don Chuy?" I asked him.

He stopped the machine and pushed up his face shield. "What do you mean?"

"What are you doing?" I repeated.

He shrugged. "Well, you guys were just talking and talking, talking, talking, talking. I wanted to see if I could make any money while you all were talking."

Chuy was an old guy who had been working there more than twenty years. The other workers respected him, and so, when they came back from lunch, they listened to what he had to say. He didn't raise his voice, and he didn't say much. But what he said convinced them to give my idea a try. "You guys can talk and complain all day—or you can give this a try like I did while you were at lunch." He paused, and then he added, "I just discovered I can double my

74

pay." His words convinced the other workers far more than anything I had said.

That old man taught me an important lesson. Before I made such a drastic change in the way the workers were paid, I should have had hard evidence to show them, based on time studies and practical examples. A few words backed up by action are far stronger than an hour-long speech.

This wasn't an isolated example in Chuy's life. Several years later, the company was moving its location to a place further up the road. I knew that Chuy walked to work, so I went to him and said, "We're moving about fifteen miles away from our current site. Are you going to be okay? Will you be able to get to work?"

He gave me that same shrug he had given me when I had asked him, years earlier, what he was doing. "I'll do what I have to do," he said. "Boss, you don't worry. I'll be at work."

A few months later, we realized we had a problem with staff tardiness and absenteeism. As our management group was discussing what to do, someone in HR said,

"Do you know we have one employee who has never missed a day of work in more than ten years?"

"Who?" I asked.

"Chuy," the HR guy said.

I should have known.

Chuy's immediate supervisor nodded. "The man gets up who-knows-how-early and takes two buses. The last one drops him about a mile from here. And every day, he's here, clocked in, and ready to start work fifteen minutes before the workday begins."

Chuy had made a pattern in his life that impressed everyone who knew him. He didn't talk much, but when he did, it was like a lion's roar: Everyone paid attention, because his actions spoke even louder than anything he ever said.

Imagine that if even 30 percent of your employees consistently let their actions speak louder than their words, and your staff was made up of doers and not talkers, the effect on your organization would be incredible.

> *The shortest answer is doing.*
> **LORD HERBERT**

ACTION-BASED LEADERSHIP

We can't expect our employees to have that level of energetic integrity if we don't demonstrate it ourselves. We can't be like parrots, mouthing a lot of empty words, and expect people to follow us. Instead, we have to be lions that only roar when they mean business.

I'm not saying there isn't a time and place for communication. When I let my employees know what we're going to do and why, they're engaged in the process, they understand what's going on, and they don't feel threatened by the changes I'm introducing. I just need to be certain that my talk is always based on practical and specific action.

If we leaders want people to listen when we talk, we need to actively demonstrate what we mean with our own lives. If we ask that our employees be respectful and loyal, we have to earn it. We do that by being certain that our actions always back up our words.

Some managers feel that employees shouldn't know any problems the organization is facing. In my opinion, though, that's bad business. Why would I want to lose the brainpower of all those people who work for me? If a hundred—or a thousand or ten thousand—people work on the same problem, odds are that, together, we'll be much better able to find a solution than I would, trying to tackle it all by myself.

CHAPTER 6
RESPECT OTHERS

When I was only eighteen, I worked as a sales manager at a printing company. The people I managed were ten to fifteen years older than I was, and to be honest, they had a lot more sales experience than I did. Despite that, I was the guy in charge of hiring and firing within my department.

One day, the owner of the company came into my office and said, "I want you to fire Bob today. He's not performing. He hasn't been making his numbers. Get rid of him."

I kind of gulped. I had a "big-boy job," but I'd only just graduated from high school. I didn't have a clue how to go about firing someone.

The owner didn't offer me any help either. All he said was, "When he comes back from lunch, go ahead and take care of it. I'm leaving now. Have a nice weekend, Aaron."

Since then, I've fired hundreds of people and, believe me, I don't do it the way I handled Bob. I pretty much did everything wrong. I sat there and let him vent for a half hour (no termination should ever last that long). I listened silently to his tears, his anger, and his frustration. Through it all, these questions kept nagging at me: Gosh, did I do everything I could for Bob? Did I do everything I was supposed to do as his manager?

I knew I'd never talked to him about his unsatisfactory performance. As a matter of fact, until the owner told me, I didn't even know that it had been unsatisfactory. What I did know was that Bob was going through a divorce. At eighteen, I didn't really understand the sort of personal challenges that went along with a marriage breaking up, but I did know that Bob was sad and that his life was hard for him.

All the while Bob was ranting, I was thinking, *I'm a leader now. People are putting their lives in my hands. Maybe these aren't life and death situations, but still, others' livelihoods are in my hands.* I knew that losing a job is terribly traumatic for anyone, let alone for someone who's already facing a serious personal issue. Termination of employment is not only a financial blow but also a blow to an individual's self-esteem.

After my experience with Bob, I made some notes to myself, which I reread often. I wrote:

Leadership means being unable to tolerate the thought of failing or seeing others fail. A leader loves his people above himself. That means he will sacrifice to ease the burdens of others. He'll make the tough decisions with the team members' best interests always first in his mind. That means he will terminate team members' employment when he sees that they'd truly be better off somewhere else. Before I fire people, I must always ask myself whether

I provided them enough opportunities to learn sufficiently and showed them respect.

Back in 1990, after my experience with Bob, I realized the importance of respect to good leadership, but I still didn't understand exactly what it means to respect others.

THE REAL MEANING OF RESPECT

Now, I'm going to fast forward in my career, from 1990 to 2010. I was now a CEO and sole owner of an organization of hundreds employees spread across three countries, and all those people were expecting me to have all the answers.

Of course, no one ever has *all* the answers. As a leader, all you can do is gather as much information as you can and then make a decision. I knew and accepted that. What I didn't know yet was that true respect for my employees might mean something very different from what I'd always believed.

If you remember, the economy wasn't doing so well back in 2010, but somehow, with a lot of hard work, my company had managed to grow by 33 percent over the previous year. I was proud of our achievement, but I was also well aware that, all around us, other companies were going under.

As a long-time sufferer of relentless dissatisfaction, I always feel I don't know enough. That means I wasn't so smug as to think that I had all the answers that would keep us from going the way of other businesses. But, I did gather enough information to know I had to do something different.

At this point, I thought my role was two-fold: figure out what that "something different" was, and give a top-down directive to make it so.

My company had gotten where it was because of my decisions and, to be quite honest, I ruled with an iron fist. I would look at the information I had, make up my mind, and announce, "Now we're going to do this. We're going to charge that hill!" My job, I believed, was to shout as I led from the front, doing my own fighting. "Charge! Now keep charging, keep charging, keeping charging!"

That approach had seemed to work fine. As I said, it was how we'd achieved the success we had, even during a recession. But now, I was starting to realize I was facing a new problem: The company had grown to the point where I couldn't be at the center of every aspect of it. I had tried to delegate some of my oversight responsibilities, but I wasn't satisfied with the results. Instead of freeing up my time, I now seemed to spend all my time telling other people what they should be doing.

Right about then, I was invited to go to Japan with a group called the Shingo Organization, which represented Toyota's lean manufacturing systems. I would have the opportunity to spend eleven or twelve days at a training facility where Toyota executives go to be trained in the Toyota production system. I was thrilled to have the opportunity, but I was also feeling pretty cocky. After all, I believed my company already practiced lean manufacturing. I'd been studying Toyota's ideas for more than six years at this point, so I didn't think I'd have much to learn.

Lean manufacturing is based on the concept of eliminating waste and creating value. The definition of waste is anything that your customer is unwilling to pay a premium for. If your customer isn't willing to pay for a particular task you're doing, then it's waste—and whatever it is, the cost of it subtracts from company earnings, reducing your profitability.

On my first day in Japan, I toured a Toyota car plant, and I found myself staring at one guy in particular as he worked. Everything he did was coordinated and precise, with a rhythm that was so fluid it seemed as though he were following a tai chi routine. Meanwhile, all the other workers seemed just as calm and focused. "That's so weird!" I said to myself.

In my experience, the manufacturing line is a place of noise and chaos. You can't get a part to fit, so you bang the heck out of it. You're missing a subcomponent, so you have to dash up and down the line looking for it. It gets pretty hectic—and it definitely doesn't have the atmosphere of a Zen meditation center.

I continued to study the line workers, trying to determine what made the difference between their attitude and the one I was accustomed to. These were young guys in their late twenties and early thirties, so I couldn't blame it on their years of experience. As I watched them, I also noticed something else: Nobody was standing over them, cracking the proverbial whip. No one was walking around making sure the workers hit their production numbers. I couldn't explain what I was seeing.

A couple of days later, I had an opportunity to spend an afternoon with Zenji Kosaka, a high-level executive at Toyota who had been trained by Taiichi Ohno, the man considered to be the founder of the Toyota production system (TPS). Mr. Kosaka, who continues to pursue the principles of TPS, is a very energetic, very intelligent, and very, very small man in his late seventies. (I'm not a particularly tall guy, but I looked huge next to him!)

As I talked with him, I began to realize that everything I'd been doing was wrong when it came to what I considered to be lean manufacturing. I'd implemented a bunch of tools, I'd created a set of charts to measure our performance, and I'd believed that it would make us incredible because, by golly, we were going to check off every single one of the boxes on those charts! It was pretty humbling to realize that I'd been on the wrong track all this time.

As I listened and learned from Mr. Kosaka, a couple questions kept nagging at me: How could I make my employees work as smoothly and independently as the workers I'd observed at the Toyota plant? How could I set up my business so that everything didn't depend on me?

"I have to be in charge of almost everything," I told Mr. Kosaka. "If I'm not in charge of everything, people don't get it done the way they should get it done. I've got to babysit people, and I'm tired of babysitting. I'm not even forty years old yet, but I don't know if I can keep doing this, because here's the truth: as long as I work eighty-five hours a week, the company is a success. But if I don't work eighty-five hours a week, we have problems. I can't even trust my financial people to watch the numbers. If I don't watch the numbers myself, next thing I know is we're losing money.

You may be familiar with the feeling I'm describing. It's frustrating and tremendously exhausting. You start losing faith in your employees' ability to think and act. You want to grab them by the shoulders and shake them! You want to ask them, "Are you going to just sit there doing nothing while the house burns down around you? Come on! Get up! Do *something*!" And instead, they just keep sitting there, waiting for you to put out the fires for them.

So as I sat there talking with Mr. Kosaka, I was at my wit's end. I knew my business was a success. I kept getting nominated for awards, and my bank and accounting firm never stopped praising my leadership. "Thank you," I'd say graciously, "thank you, thank you," but inside, I was terrified, because I knew the company was growing so fast that it was about to hit a brick wall. I couldn't do any more than

I was doing. And that meant we couldn't grow any bigger than we already were, because there was just no way I could handle any more. I was the brick wall.

Another problem I'd run into that year was that whenever I moved a key leadership team to another plant, the new plant's performance would shoot up within a week or two, but the old plant's performance would drop at just about the same rate. The team had the same problem I had. Without direct oversight, everything fell apart.

Mr. Kosaka listened to me describe what was going on, and then he asked, "Do you know what respect is?"

Well, of course, I knew what respect was! "It's treating people the way you want to be treated," I told him. "In the West, it's called the Golden Rule."

He shook his head. "That is not respect."

I tried again. "It's when people show you the courtesy you deserve."

He shook his head again. "No, that is not respect."

"Where I come from," I said, starting to feel frustrated, "it's a street term that means, 'Don't mess with me, or I will hurt you.'"

"That is not how I understand respect," Mr. Kosaka said.

I scratched my head and came up with still another definition of respect, and Mr. Kosaka said, "No, that is not respect."

I was getting irritated. I kept thinking of different ways to explain to him what I meant, but, every time, he just shook his head and told me, "That is not respect."

Eventually, I lost my temper. I slammed my hands on the table and said, "So what is respect? Do you even know?"

He nodded. "I do know what respect is."

"I don't think you do," I told him, "because I've given great definitions and you keep saying no."

"I know exactly what respect is," he said.

"Then tell me," I said. "What is it? What is it?"

"Respect is this," he said. "Never, ever, ever, ever do anything for any group or individual that they're capable of doing for themselves. That is the only definition of respect." He was silent for a moment, letting his words sink in, and then he added, "When you do not act that way, you enslave people. You take away their self-esteem. You take away their self-worth, and you make them dependent on you for everything."

I had nothing to say in reply. Mr. Kosaka's simple explanation had turned upside down everything I believed about leadership.

As I flew home from Japan, new ideas were bouncing around in my head. I knew that I had never let my employees learn and grow through failure. Instead, I had subjected them all to my will, my thoughts, my ideas. I had done things for them they were capable of doing themselves. I was frustrated that everything was on my shoulders, but I was the one who had insisted on carrying that load myself and never letting anyone else share it. My employees should have been operating as a collaborative group of minds trying to solve multiple problems. Instead, almost everything depended on one guy—who wasn't actually all that smart and certainly didn't have all the answers—trying to solve all the problems.

It was a long flight home, but I was awake for the entire trip. I felt like a failure. I even wondered if I should step down from the CEO position and hire someone else to take my place. My employees had entrusted me with their livelihoods, and I had let them down. I had never respected their free agency, their innate right to make decisions and live with the consequences of those decisions.

When I finally reached my home, I was tired and cranky, but it was a Saturday morning, and my kids were going strong. As I lay on the sofa, trying to take a nap, they were running around like little maniacs.

"Daddy, Daddy!" Olivia shouted. "Make me cereal!"

She was only four at the time, and I knew it wasn't her fault I was exhausted, so I heaved a big sigh and pulled myself up off the sofa. "Yeah, yeah," I mumbled. "Sure thing, just give me a minute."

I went into the kitchen and started getting out all the things I needed to "make cereal"—a bowl, a spoon, the milk from the refrigerator, a box of cereal out of the cupboard. I was so tired I was half-asleep on my feet, and as I stood there, ready to pour the cereal into the bowl, I had a flashback to another bowl of cereal I'd poured long, long ago, back when I was four years old.

As a little kid, I was an early riser. On weekends, my parents wanted to sleep in, but every Saturday, little Aaron would jump on their bed, because he wanted to eat cereal while he watched cartoons. Finally, my mother took me into the kitchen and said, "Aaron, do you know how to get your own cereal?"

Well, obviously I didn't. I was only four years old! But, my mom didn't seem to think that was a good enough excuse. She said, "Aaron, where's the cereal?"

I knew where the cereal was kept, so I went and got a box of Wheaties out of the cupboard.

"Where are the bowls?" my mom asked me next. "Can you go get one?"

Yup, I knew where the bowls lived, so I stood on tiptoe, grabbed my favorite bowl from the cupboard, and gave it to my mother. She set it on the table, and then she asked, "What else do you need to eat cereal, Aaron?"

I looked at the bowl and the box of cereal, and then I said, "A spoon!"

She nodded. "Where are the spoons?"

I couldn't actually reach the drawer where the spoons were kept, so she gave me a boost and helped me get a spoon out.

"Now what?" she asked.

"Milk!"

"And where do we keep the milk?"

I went to the refrigerator and opened the door, but the gallon of milk was too heavy for a four-year-old to lift.

"From now on," my mother said, "I'll buy smaller jugs of milk so you can lift them, Aaron." Then she brought the milk to the table and said, "Today, Aaron, I'm going to show you how to make your own breakfast. And then tonight, I'll leave your bowl and your cereal and your spoon right here on the table. When you get up in the morning, they'll be waiting for you. All you'll have to do is pour your cereal in the bowl—and then go to the refrigerator, get the milk, and pour that on top of the cereal. Okay?"

I nodded. I was feeling excited, because making my own breakfast seemed like such a grown-up thing to do.

"Okay then," my mother said. "Now I'm going to show you how to turn on the TV."

From then on, every weekend morning, my cereal and bowl would be waiting for me on the table when I got up. I'd pour my cereal into the bowl, get the milk, pour it, and finally, very carefully, carry it into the living room, where I'd sit in front of the television while I ate.

As I got older and grew taller, my mother no longer needed to get out anything for me the night before. I continued my habit of waking up early on weekend mornings, but I didn't bother my parents. I let them sleep as long as they wanted while I happily chewed my cereal and watched cartoons.

My mom, I'm sure, didn't know the definition of respect that Mr. Kosaka gave me, but she did understand the concept of making her children self-reliant and self-sufficient. As I grew, she continued to teach me new ways to be independent. I didn't appreciate the favor she had done me until I moved out for the first time and had roommates who didn't know how to cook, didn't know how to do laundry, and didn't know how to sew a button on. I knew how to take care of myself, and it felt good.

As I stood there that day so many years later, swaying on my feet with exhaustion, I realized that my mom had shown me the kind of respect that Mr. Kosaka was talking about. She hadn't given me all the answers. Instead, she had helped me see that I could do things for myself.

I put the cereal box down on the counter. "Olivia!" I called. "Come here! I'm going to teach you how to make your own cereal."

> *Every person has an inborn worth and can contribute to the human community. We all can treat one another with dignity and respect, provide opportunities to grow toward our fullest lives, and help one another discover and develop our unique gifts. We each deserve this, and we all can extend it to others.*
>
> **AUTHOR UNKNOWN**

MAKE THE WORLD A BETTER PLACE

As leaders, we'd like to know that by the time we leave this world, we will have done something that has improved the lives of others in some way. We usually think in terms of something we do when, actually, the very best things we can do for others is to give *them* the power to improve their own lives. When we fail to do that, we rob them of their self-esteem. We steal their free agency. We subjugate them to our will because, deep down, we don't feel they're capable of doing things on their own. We fail to show them respect.

Years after my first trip to Japan, I went back with a group of employees from Mexico, including my plant manager, Iliana Rivera. Iliana is wonderful leader, but on this particular day, she was feeling pretty stressed. At the end of a class that we attended with Mr. Kosaka, she stood up and said, "Kosaka-sensei, I have a situation. Our sales for this month are falling short. We're not going to have enough to cover our overhead. What do you do in situations like this?"

Mr. Kosaka looked at her for a moment, and then said, "Thank you so much for sharing this concern with me." He gave her a gentle smile, and then he was quiet for so long that we all started to think that that was going to be his only response. Finally, he said, "I'm going to ask you a question. Is there anyone in this room who shares this problem with you? Anyone who will also be impacted by this problem?"

"Yeah," Iliana said, "this affects everybody."

"Will you please point to the people it affects?"

She started going around the room, pointing, but he stopped her and said, "Please say each person by name, and then tell me how that person is impacted by your problem." He turned to the rest of the room. "Please stand up when your name is said."

Iliana started out with Juan. "He manages a department with forty employees and he'll probably lose 20 percent of his employees because we won't be able to afford them." She turned next to Elena. "She is head of engineering, and we need to hire five more engineers. But Elena won't be able to do that, because we don't have the money to pay them." One by one, Iliana went around the room, pointing to people and explaining how each person was going to be affected. I could hear the stress in her voice, and I knew how anxious she was feeling.

Finally, she pointed at me. "Señor Aaron will be affected, because he's the owner of the company. When we lose money, it's his money we're losing."

Every person in the room was standing up now. Mr. Kosaka nodded. "How lucky you are to have a group of people like this to share that problem with you."

And that was it. He didn't offer us any advice. He didn't say, "Well, listen, here's what I'd do if I were in your place." Instead, he showed us ourselves.

We all met that afternoon, and together we solved the problem. Everyone came up with ideas on how to get sales—and we had sales by the next day. I'm not saying we got rich overnight, but we had enough to keep us going until sales picked up again.

That year proved to be one of the best years in the history of our company, and I always thank Mr. Kosaka for our success. He made us recognize that solving the problem was our responsibility, and he made us see our own power to do that. He showed us respect. And because he did, he made our world a whole lot better.

PRACTICE RESPECT!

I've been fortunate throughout my life to be allowed to learn and fail and grow, and yet, as a leader, I've often taken that privilege away from the people I lead. As a parent, I've also denied my children this opportunity. Like many parents, I've not wanted my children to repeat the same mistakes I made.

But learning doesn't work like that. For example, children have been touching hot items since a caveman made the first fire. Parents can warn children not to touch a hot object until they're blue in the face, but the only way to learn not to touch something hot is to touch something hot. Kids can't bypass the learning process. When we don't show people respect, we bypass the learning process.

Before you can make this kind of respect a habit, you'll need to practice it, over and over. I don't claim to be totally consistent about doing this yet (especially with my children). I have had a lifetime of acting in a different way, and I catch myself falling back into old habits. I don't always succeed at practicing respect the way I want to.

But I don't look at these backward slips as failures. Not succeeding isn't the same as failing. Failing, in my opinion, is not getting back up and trying again. I always try again. I get up every day and remind myself to never, ever, ever do anything for any group or individual that they're capable of doing for themselves. That's respect.

Somebody once asked Gentleman Jim, the heavy-weight champion, "To become a champion, what do you have to do?"

He answered, "Fight one more round. When your feet are so tired that you have to shuffle back to the center of the ring, fight one more round. When your arms are so tired that you can hardly lift your hands to come on guard, fight one more round. When your nose is bleeding and your eyes are black and you are so tired you wish your opponent would crack you one on the jaw and put you to sleep, fight one more round—remembering that the man who always fights one more round is never whipped."

CHAPTER 7

LOVE CHANGE

Remember the Dr. Seuss book *Green Eggs and Ham*? The little boy in the story is convinced that he will never, ever like green eggs and ham (not in a house, not with a mouse; not in a box, not with a fox; and not in any situation whatsoever). Eventually, though, Sam-I-Am persuades the boy to try the dish Sam-I-Am is offering—and the boy discovers that he *does* like green eggs and ham.

I've never tried to persuade any of my children to eat green eggs and ham, but I'm very familiar with the same sort of attitude when it comes to foods they don't like. For example, my son Jack has told me many times that he doesn't like mushrooms.

"But have you tried them?" I ask.

"Yes," he insists, "I have. And I didn't like them."

"But maybe you could learn to like them. Maybe you'd like them if you tried them again."

"Nope." He's absolutely sure about it. "I don't like mushrooms, and I will never like mushrooms. Mushrooms are *disgusting*!"

Anyone who's been a parent knows the frustration of trying to convince a kid to change his mind about food. As adults, though, we're not always all that different.

For example, I never used to like brussels sprouts. My mom cooked them when I was a kid, and every time, the entire house would smell like rotting cabbage for days afterward. I hated the things. Then, a couple years ago, I asked the waiter at a restaurant what he recommended, and he said, "Oh, you have to try our brussels sprouts."

I made a face. "No sir, I'll eat anything, but I don't eat brussels sprouts." I *will*, literally, eat anything. Guinea pig, stomach, frog, snake, beef tongue, horse meat, and intestine are all some of my favorite dishes.

As I said that, all of sudden I felt like a hypocrite. Every year, when I take a group of employees to Japan, I take them to my favorite sushi restaurant and ask them to order something, and a lot of the time, they'll say, "Sorry, Aaron, I don't eat fish. I hate fish."

"Have you ever had good fish?" I'll ask.

"Yeah," they'll say. "My mom used to make fish all the time. It was gross."

There are some things we just never outgrow! But I keep asking questions. "Why was it gross?"

"It just was. I didn't like the taste."

If you want to reach whatever is at the root of a problem, you can't stop after the first or second question you ask; you have to keep going. I've found that I need to ask at least five questions before I start to reach the root cause, so I always keep pushing. We call it the **five whys**. Ask "Why?" five times to get to the root of a problem.

"But why did it taste gross?" I ask.

"I don't know. It just did."

"What kind of fish did your mom make?"

"I don't know . . . Mrs. Paul's or, maybe Van de Kamp's."

"So your mom made fish sticks?"

"Yeah."

Now, no offense to anyone's mom, but heating up frozen fish sticks in the oven is not even close to the fresh sushi made by Japan's expert chefs.

"Do you know why those fish sticks tasted gross?" I ask next.

"Because fish is gross."

At this point, I might as well be talking to Jack! But I don't give up. "Fish sticks taste gross," I say, "because they're not real fish. They're all the bad parts of the fish, the parts that are too old or slimy to sell any other way, ground up into little bits and pressed together in a stick."

"Oh."

"So, you don't like bad fish. But, you don't know if you like good fish, because you've never had it. Now, let's go try some sushi."

Many of my employees have never been in a sushi restaurant before. When I take them there, I push them outside their familiar comfort zones. But they go, and they try sushi—and pretty much everyone walks out saying, "Oh my gosh, that was amazing. I can't believe how delicious that was. Every piece was so good. Once I forgot that it was raw fish, it tasted so good."

So all that was running through my head as the waiter stood there waiting for me to decide what to order. I thought, *You know what, Aaron? You haven't eaten brussels sprouts since you were probably nine years old. Try the dang brussels sprouts.*

So I did, and I discovered that they don't boil sprouts anymore. They grill them in bacon fat with a little bit of balsamic vinegar. They're spectacular when they're made that way. In fact, I love them. I order them whenever I eat out. They've become one of my favorite side dishes. But, I never would have discovered that if I hadn't been willing to change my eating habits—and try something new.

COMFORTABLE HABITS

Kids may resist new foods, but they're usually far more open to other changes than we adults are. We've lived so many more years than they have, and in the process, we've formed ingrained habits.

"I sleep on the right side of the bed," a friend of mine told me. "I can't get comfortable if I try to sleep on the left side. I *have* to sleep on the right side of the bed."

"For the rest of your life?" I asked him.

He nodded. "For the rest of my life."

"But, maybe if you tried it, you'd find you liked the left side of the bed. Who knows what you've been missing all these years?"

He shook his head. "No, I have to sleep on the right side of the bed. Otherwise, I don't sleep."

I could see his mind was made up, so I dropped the conversation and left him to his right-side-of-the-bed sleeping habit. After all, who cares what side of the bed someone sleeps on, right? But, an unwillingness to change can have far more serious effects on our lives than we might suspect.

"I've run my company this way for the past twenty years," an older executive told me once. "It's always worked fine. Why would I want to change things now?"

I knew this man was in trouble. What's more, his business was in trouble—and he was unwilling to see that fixing the problem was going to require that he change the way he did things. Instead, he blamed other people while he continued exactly as he had before, insisting that what worked ten years ago *should* work now, no matter what.

I suspect all of us have felt like that CEO at one time or another. We've grown familiar with the way we do things, and when we find that other people are no longer going along with our methods, we put the blame on them. We want *them* to adjust their behavior, never suspecting that we're the ones who need to change.

Or, maybe you think you've achieved everything you ever wanted, and now you just want to maintain your position. You're worried that if you change something, even something small, everything will fall apart, and you'll lose it all. But here's the thing: If you refuse to change, you can't grow. You can't learn anything new; you can't explore new territory; you can't make amazing discoveries.

> *It may be hard for an egg to turn into a bird: It would be a jolly sight harder for it to learn to fly while remaining an egg. We are like eggs at present. And you cannot go on indefinitely being just an ordinary, decent egg. We must be hatched or go bad.*
> **C. S. LEWIS**

RESISTING CHANGE

It's human nature to resist change. Change pushes us out of our comfort zones into unfamiliar territory. No one likes to give up being comfortable, but it's not just that. We're afraid that unknown perils may lurk in this new frontier. We worry that we won't be strong enough or smart enough or skilled enough to handle new dangers we've never had to face before.

For children, however, change is simply a part of life. Last year, they were four feet tall and wore size 4 shoes. This year, they're six inches taller, and they're wearing size 6s. This year they're in fourth grade and have Mr. Wilson for a teacher, but next year they know they'll be in fifth with Mrs. Smith. Some of these changes aren't easy. You may outgrow your favorite shoes—and Mr. Wilson might be a lot nicer than Mrs. Smith. But, kids know it's pointless to resist. Change just keeps happening. And, a lot of the time, kids look forward to those changes. They anticipate the day when they'll be old enough to be allowed to stay home alone—or drive—or go to college. Not only do they take these changes in stride, but they celebrate them.

So here's a challenge: What if, instead of thinking of change as something bad, something that makes our life harder, we practice thinking of change as growth?

CHANGE IS GOOD

We've already talked about the need to continually ask ourselves, "Does this still work? And if not, why?" We can't ask those questions, not with any sort of integrity, if we're not genuinely prepared to change whenever the answer is, "No, this *doesn't* still work."

Our resistance to change may be what makes us reluctant to ask those difficult questions—but we're kidding ourselves if we think we can avoid change by not asking them. Change is going to happen anyway, one way or another.

Let's say your doctor tells you that you're overweight and you're heading toward a heart attack if you don't lose weight. You have two choices: listen to your doctor and change your lifestyle by dieting and exercising—or do nothing. Dieting and exercise aren't easy, and you might take the short-term perspective: "I like eating. I don't like exercise. Dieting means I can't eat what I want, and exercise means I have to do something I don't like. They're both uncomfortable, and I don't want to be uncomfortable. So I'm not going to change."

Meanwhile, though, if you do nothing, your body is going to change anyway—but not for the better. As your overweight body becomes obese, you get diabetes. You have joint problems. Your heart condition grows worse. Now, your ability to move around becomes limited. You have to give up your long-term goals, because your health won't allow you to achieve them. Eventually, your life may even come to an end far sooner than you ever anticipated. You refused to make short-term sacrifices at the cost of your long-term quality of life.

When it comes to the business world, the same principles apply. We sometimes avoid change simply because it requires a little effort and discomfort, but in the long run, the short-term discomfort is well worth the long-term payoffs.

CHANGE VERSUS BOREDOM

Imagine if nothing ever changed. Every day the sun shone. Every day we did exactly the same things and ate exactly the same foods. Every day we talked to the same people and went to the same places. After a while, it would get pretty boring.

Whether we realize it or not, we all need new challenges in our lives and in our work. When we don't have them, we lose interest in what's going on around us.

Every now and then I notice an employee who's no longer acting the same as he used to. His job performance gets worse and worse, and finally, I sit down with him and say, "Hey, you're doing a terrible job. What's going on?"

A lot of times, here's what he says, "I dread coming to work. I'm bored out of my mind. I've been running on cruise control for years now, and I'm sick of my work."

As leaders, we need to make sure our people are being challenged enough to grow. We need to give them opportunities to change. Of course, change purely for the sake of change can be destructive, but everyone, adults just as much as kids, needs the opportunity to grow and experience new things.

FORWARD—OR BACKWARD

One of the greatest employees I've ever had started out as a junior draftsman in the engineering department when he was about nineteen years old and then became a rising star who worked his way up through the company. Anything we gave him to do he took on and learned everything he could about the new challenge. He moved around the company, and in the process, he gained skills in many areas from computer programming to security compliance, from engineering to purchasing.

Eventually, he became the director of purchasing, where he oversaw a spending budget of $75 to $80 million a year. He was now a member of the company's senior leadership team, a dependable go-to guy. He probably felt as though he'd "made it," he'd reached his ultimate professional goal.

Sadly, this meant he was no longer constantly growing. Instead, I watched him stagnate. Meanwhile, the company was going through three or four years of tremendous growth, but he was no longer keeping pace. One day, he woke up and realized he had nothing to offer the company. He'd become obsolete.

"I don't know what happened," he told me. "I feel like the rest of you are so far in front of me, I could never catch up." I didn't terminate his employment. He made the decision to leave on his own. "I can't stay in a job where I'm not contributing anything," he said.

I've learned that it's always a mistake when I don't continually set new challenges for the people I lead. Now, I always tell my employees, "I'm going to give you a new challenge. Here's what I expect to see. Here's how I think it should look when you've accomplished it."

If I challenge them with a skill set in which they have 0 percent proficiency, they will have to make a tremendous effort to reach 90 percent proficiency. It's going to take time, but they will feel really, really good once they reach that 90 percent mark (because, after all, a 90 is an A just as much as a 100 is).

At 90 percent proficiency, people tend to shift into cruise control. I hear people say things such as "My job is so easy for me. I go to work, and I don't have to even think about what I'm doing. I can finally relax at work because everything runs so smoothly. I know exactly what I'm doing. What a great feeling!"

I've found that getting people to move from 90 percent to 100 percent proficiency takes far more effort than was needed to get them from 0 to 90. From 90 to 100 it's all about the small nuances: the slight bend of your wrist when you're shooting a basket, the tighter arm on your golf backswing. And then, face it, you'll never actually reach 100 percent proficiency, because as we've already said, perfection is impossible. So very few people have the self-discipline to even try.

In the business setting, the reality is that we probably don't need our workers to achieve anything more than a 90 percent proficiency in their skills sets. At 90 percent, an organization is already doing incredibly well. So that's great, but you still don't want to see stagnated workers. As a leader, what I always say when I see someone get to that 90 percent mark is this: "It's time for a change. Now I'm going to move you to another position that will put you back to 0 percent—and I expect you to become as proficient at it as you are at your current position."

No one likes me too much when I do this. People prefer to be on cruise control, at least at first. They like feeling that their job requires no effort from them, and they don't appreciate me coming along and making a change that makes no sense in their minds.

"My job is to help you learn and grow," I tell them. "That's my biggest responsibility to you. And you are not learning and growing anymore—so I'm going to give you your next challenge."

This management style may not work for your line of work, but you need to find a technique that *will* work to keep your people from coming to work on cruise control.

Nothing remains at rest. You're either moving forward, or you're moving backward, either growing or decaying. Staying in one place is stagnation—and something that's stagnant is dead. According to a law of physics, an object in motion tends to remain in motion, but that doesn't necessarily mean it's going forward. When it comes to most human beings, after hitting that 90 percent proficiency wall, they remain stationery for a very, very short moment, and then they bounce off it. Now, instead of moving forward, they're moving backward. That's when careers end. When it's an organization-wide problem, companies fail and go out of business.

LOWER THE WATER LEVEL

Imagine for a moment that you're on a ship floating on the ocean. You look over the railing and see only water. What you don't realize is that just five inches beneath your hull lies a long ridge of jagged rocks. The water is flat and calm, though, and your ship floats smoothly over the rocks.

And then a storm comes up out of nowhere, as they do, sometimes, at sea. Suddenly, that flat, peaceful ocean has turned into swelling waves and deep troughs. Your ship rides an enormous wave up . . . up . . . up . . . and then down, down, down! You hold on tight to the railing, and what do you see now when you look overboard? You see that line of enormous, sharp rocks, ready to tear a hole in the ship's hull.

How does that apply to the way we feel about change? As long as things are going smoothly, we assume that everything is fine, and no change is needed. Sometimes, we need to intentionally lower the water level, so that we can see what's lurking beneath the surface. Then, we can crush those rocks *before* the storm hits, and the next time our ship is rocked by waves, we'll have nothing to fear, because we will already have dealt with the problem.

This can require taking action in a variety of ways. It might mean, for example, we insist that our most skilled worker take a month's vacation *before* she gets burned out, instead of waiting until there's a problem.

If she's our most skilled worker, though, we may think we can't let her take a vacation because if she does, her entire department is going to stop running smoothly. Well, if that's the case, then good— better you "lower the water" and find out where your weak points are than wait until your best worker takes a job somewhere else because she's too exhausted to keep going. Better to deal with the rocks when the water is calm—when your employee is only on vacation, not gone for good—than to wait for a crisis to hit. So, don't wait until the employee's doing a terrible job or decides to leave. Fix the situation before it gets to that point!

I've heard my employees say, "Aaron loves to stir the pot." When I notice that things are going really smoothly in a certain department, I decide to make a change that will disrupt things. I don't do it to mess with people's heads or just to stir things up for the heck of it. I'm lowering the water to see if there are any hidden dangers I should be aware of lurking beneath the surface.

I might say to someone, "You're doing an incredible job in accounts payable, so incredible, in fact, that I'm going put you in customer service."

That person usually responds with something like this: "What? I don't know anything about customer service! Why would you move me there if I'm doing a good job here in accounts payable? I don't want to move."

"Yeah," I say, "I think you do. If you can do a good job where you are now, I'm confident you'll be able to learn whatever it takes to be good in customer service. You'll have fun, I promise—and the more skills you learn, the more valuable you'll be to our company. If you're multitalented, I can deploy you in more areas if we should run into a crisis."

Sometimes, I use the game of chess as an analogy when I'm asking employees to change their positions in the company. "Look," I say, "you're like a knight on the chessboard. You're a valuable piece to have, but if you could be a knight, a bishop, and a rook, think how much more value you'd have. Man, people will pay big money for you then."

As a business leader, you will need to make changes to processes as well as people. Don't wait for the moment when everything is falling apart and nothing is working anymore. Instead, when the water is smooth and calm, ask yourself what would happen if your company stopped doing things this way. What if this process were eliminated? Do you really need it? This goes back to the *why* question we talked about earlier in this book. If we can't say in one sentence why we're doing something the way we do, if it requires an entire book to explain our reasons for doing it, then we need to seriously consider that we may not need to do it at all.

Making a habit of asking why—and being prepared to change in response to the answer—isn't a once-a-quarter, let's-have-a-big-day sort of thing. Instead, it should be a daily habit. It should be ingrained, not only in the way you lead but also in your entire corporate culture.

GRADUAL CHANGE

The change we ask of ourselves and our employees doesn't have to always be huge and sudden. Just as the Japanese principle of kaizen relies on small, incremental improvements, sometimes the tiniest changes, one after the other, can be the most effective. If you're weight training, for example, you don't suddenly throw an extra forty-five-pound weight on the bar. You add one pound, then five, then maybe ten, and little by little, a day at a time, you build up your strength until the day when you find that lifting that extra forty-five pounds is something you can easily do.

When you think of change this way—not as something huge and threatening, but as an opportunity to learn and grow—then your attitude toward change—well, it changes! Change becomes something to anticipate. It's something that makes life seem bigger, more satisfying. And when this sort of change is integrated into your workday, it makes work become more satisfying too. You'll feel as though you're accomplishing something that matters, not just going through the same old routines over and over. There's an exhilaration about it. It makes work fun!

> *Mediocrity is easy. Stay away from easy.*
> **SCOTT ALEXANDER**

CHANGE VERSUS MEDIOCRITY

If you're unwilling to get on board with these ideas—if you resist all change at all costs—then you're settling for mediocrity. There are very few things in life that I'd say I truly hate, but I truly hate mediocrity.

Several years ago, an attractive young woman with a big personality, cocky and smart as can be, worked in my accounting department. Let's call her Amy. I was keeping an eye on Amy, the way I do with all my employees, and I'd started to notice some things that concerned me. When I sat down with her immediate supervisor and asked for her perspective, I learned that Amy had started out strong but then had seemed to hit a wall. She was no longer getting better at her job while, at the same time, she was often late on Monday mornings because she'd been partying all weekend. On Friday afternoons, she would make excuses to leave early. Clearly, Amy's mind was no longer focused on her work.

I didn't do anything at first. I just kept watching her, hoping she would be able to get herself back on track. The more I observed her, the more I found myself thinking, This is a talented woman. *She has the ability to really do a lot of things, but she's content to be mediocre at everything. Her life is going nowhere.*

I'm sure Amy didn't see things the same way. Most likely, she was getting a lot of attention in her personal life, and that had become the crutch she was leaning on to make herself feel as though she was actually going somewhere.

Then, one day, an important report from the accounting department didn't land on my desk when I'd expected it. When I went to find out what had happened, I discovered that it hadn't even been begun. I wasn't especially happy about that. In fact, I was jumping down the accounting manager's throat, yelling, "Why was this not done on time? Who was responsible for getting it done?"

The head of the accounting department looked unhappy, but all she said was, "It's my fault, Aaron. I'm the boss, so if something doesn't get done in my department, it's my fault."

I stopped yelling and started thinking (which is always a smart thing to do). "Tell me the name of the individual who was responsible for completing this report," I said. I had a sinking feeling that I knew the name she was going to say.

Sure enough, it was Amy. I called her into my office, and we sat down to talk. She seemed totally unfazed, completely unconcerned. She wasn't disrespectful to me, but her attitude told me loud and clear that she couldn't care less about the work she did for me. In fact, I sensed mediocrity oozing from her every pore.

Finally, I leaned back in my chair, and I said, "Amy, I'm going to do you an enormous favor today. Honestly, it's going to change your life. You're going to look back and say, 'Wow, that was one of the greatest days in my life.'"

"Really?" For the first time since we'd been talking, I saw a flicker of interest pass over her face. "What're you going to do?"

I leaned forward and said, "Amy, go back to your desk and pack up. And then I want you to go down to HR and tell them that you're quitting right here, right now."

She gave a nervous little giggle, as if she thought I was joking.

"I'm dead serious, Amy," I said. "Quit. Leave. Get out of here." She wasn't smiling now, but she still hadn't moved. "Don't make me fire you. Have enough dignity to walk out of here on your own terms. Quit right now."

"But why?"

"Because I am sick and tired of sitting here watching you swim around in the pool of mediocrity you built for yourself, not fulfilling one of the talents that you've been given." I stood up and went to the door, but before I opened it, I said, "I can't stop you from being mediocre, Amy, but I don't have to let you take a seat from somebody else who wants to learn and grow, someone who actually wants to do something productive in this life."

Her eyes filled up with tears. "You're being so mean, Aaron."

I went back and leaned against my desk. "No, Amy. I'm not being mean. I'm probably not being nice, but I am being kind." I handed her a tissue so she could blow her nose. "A kind person wants to help people so that they're willing to do whatever is necessary to learn and grow. Nice people say silly little things that aren't true so they don't hurt feelings. My job, Amy, is not to be nice to you. My job is to be kind. My job is to help you learn and grow. Please go pack your stuff up and quit. Do not make me fire you. I have almost no respect left for you. The little bit I have will be maintained if you act like an adult by getting up and leaving this office, and then packing your stuff and getting out."

By now, she was crying so hard I couldn't shove her out the door where everyone else would see her face. So I let her cry while

I sat down at my desk again and started doing some work. After a few minutes, she sniffed, blew her nose, and said, "Nobody has ever spoken to me that way."

"That's too bad," I said. "Maybe they should have."

She finally left my office, and I asked HR to give her a two-weeks' severance check. And that was that.

Or at least that's what I thought.

Amy surprised me by coming back to my office later that afternoon. "I'm not going to quit," she announced.

I sighed. "Okay. Then I guess I'll have to fire you."

"No," she said, "please don't. You're right about me, but I'm not going to be mediocre anymore. I'm going to change."

So I gave her another chance—and I didn't regret it. She did change. In fact, her work improved so much that, a year later, we promoted her to a better position. Another year after that we made her into a manager, and she oversaw a huge department. She was a superstar. I was so proud of her. I like to think that when I confronted her with the truth about herself, I lowered the water level so that she could see the rocks that were hiding beneath the surface of her fun-loving, party-girl life. Once she saw the truth, she was able to become the person she was capable of being.

Mediocrity can feel good sometimes. It can feel comfortable and easy. But it gets in the way of our becoming who we're really meant to be. Once we discover what's possible, the way Amy did, being mediocre no longer seems so good. It's like settling for a constant diet of McDonald's cheeseburgers when we've been offered gourmet meals.

When we refuse to change, we're forced to settle for mediocrity. We can't excel at anything if we're not willing to face challenges and allow them to change us. Amy thought that having fun in her social life was more important than doing her best on her job, but she discovered that what makes life *really* fun is allowing yourself to be changed into a better person than you've ever been before.

Ultimately, it's about your attitude toward life. It's easy not to notice some of the challenges to change that come along. Believe me, I know. We automatically say, "No thank you," whenever we're offered brussels sprouts—or sushi or green eggs and ham. We *know* we don't like what's being offered. But when we open our minds to the possibility of change, we open up our lives to a bigger world, a world full of new skills, new pleasures, new achievements. We become bigger people living bigger lives.

As a leader, that's the challenge I want to offer my employees, and that's the challenge I want to take on for myself too. If I were telling Jack one more thing he needs to do to be heir to the throne, it's the challenge he'd have to accept for himself—and it's the challenge I'm giving you, as well.

> *One key to successful leadership is continuous personal change. Personal change is a reflection of our inner growth and empowerment.*
>
> **ROBERT E. QUINN**

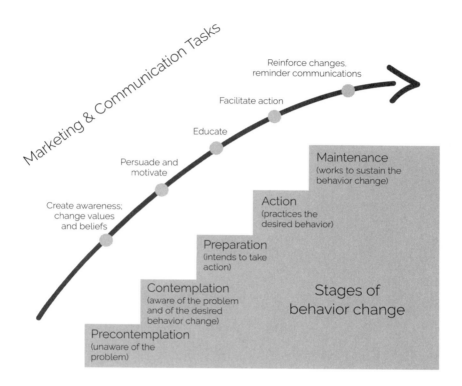

James Prochaska and Carlo DiClemente created the transtheoretical stages of change model that's diagrammed here. The steps outline the inner tasks involved with change, while the line above indicates how leaders can motivate their organization to engage in change.

CHAPTER 8

YEARN TO LEARN

few years ago, those of us who lived in Las Vegas watched the construction of a building called the Harmon. It was planned to be a combination hotel, spa, and condo complex; a forty-nine-story tower that was going to part of the CityCenter development, a sixty-seven-acre, eighteen-million-square-foot, $8.5 billion project that, at the time, was being called the largest private real estate development in US history. The Harmon was going to be an oval-shaped tower with about four hundred rooms and two hundred condos.

Construction began in 2007, and floor by floor, we watched the building go up. But then, in July 2008, after about half the building had gone up, construction stopped. We wondered what had happened, and eventually, we found out that an engineer working on the project had discovered that the reinforcing bars within the structure were either missing or improperly installed. This issue meant that the building lacked structural integrity. If it were subjected to an earthquake or high winds, it could easily topple.

The developers wanted to salvage what they could of their project—nearly $300 million had already been spent—so they decided to reduce the originally planned forty-nine floors to twenty-eight floors. The *Las Vegas Sun* wrote in February 2009, "The incredible shrinking Harmon seems unfortunately fated to look like a stubby, squashed stepchild next to its soaring CityCenter siblings."

But even the shortened version of the building came to a halt. For a while, it sat there empty. Finally, in 2014, the building we had watched go up floor by floor now went down, floor by floor. Because it was so close to its more successful neighbors, its demolition had to be done slowly, one floor at a time, over the space of nearly a year. By 2015, all that was left of the Harmon Tower was a slab of cement on the ground.

LEARNING AS STRUCTURE

I've seen something similar happen with businesses. They start out big. They hit $5 million, and then they reach $10 million. But they can't make it to $20 million. Instead, little by little, they slide backward, until they're gone, forgotten. Why? Because, like the Harmon Tower, they lack the integral strength they needed to support their growth. They didn't invest in the structure that would hold up the weight of their company.

A commitment to learning is the most fundamental organizational structure all businesses need. Every time my business has become stagnant, unable to push through to the next level of growth, it's always been because we had a learning problem. As soon I strengthened our learning structure again—*boom!* We'd break through from

$20 million to $40 million . . . and then to $80 million, $100 million, and even higher.

When I say I strengthened our learning structure, what I'm saying is that I invested hard dollars in my own learning as well as that of my employees. We went to conferences. We read books and have a book club that rewards people for learning. I brought in the authors of some of those books to help us reach deeper levels of understanding. We learned new systems and theories. We continue to pay for education and advanced degrees. We run a university where our people can get their basic elementary education, high school GED, and learn about Lean, a second language, negotiation skills, Toyota Way, Shingo Model, best hiring practices, leadership, basic computer skills, and more. We send people around the world to study different companies. I personally have taken over one hundred employees to Japan to do study tours with Toyota and do the deep work to truly acquire knowledge. We tour companies so we can learn from them and share what knowledge we have.

But I didn't start with all that. I started with buying books and reading them, then sharing them with my team and discussing them chapter by chapter. Learning can be very inexpensive, but it's essential to growing a business.

> *Get over the idea that only children should spend their time in study. Be a student so long as you still have something to learn, and this will mean all your life.*
> **HENRY L. DOHERTY**

KNOW WHAT YOU DON'T KNOW

Whenever I'm faced with a new situation that challenges me, I ask myself, "What don't I know? What is it I don't understand? What piece of knowledge am I missing to overcome this?"

I always tell my employees one of the biggest strengths of our company is that we have a CEO who's not that smart. It's true that I am not the smartest guy in the world, but I do know something very clearly: I don't know what I don't know. Knowing this has forced me, throughout my career, to go out there and learn. I ask myself if there is a better way. Who's doing it better? Can I copy it? Can I learn from them? Can I copy them until I figure it out, until I understand it so well that I can change and apply it exactly the way we need to do it?

When I think I have the right answer, I ask: Why *shouldn't* I do it? I don't say I am going to do it and look for evidence to support my idea. I purposefully go to prove why I shouldn't do it. That simple change in mind-set has saved me many times from allowing emotion to trump logic. Don't be afraid to question your own decision to make sure it is right.

Becoming successful isn't something that happens by chance. You don't just wake up one day and discover a miracle has happened that's turned your business into a success. It takes deliberate effort. To go back to the weight-lifting metaphor I used in the last chapter, if I lie around on the sofa all day thinking about my muscles, they are never going to get any bigger, no matter how much hard thinking I do. Instead, I have to take the weights off the rack, lock my elbows, take a deep breath, let the weights down slowly—and then, with an explosive exhale, push the weights up off my chest. That's the only way my muscles are going to get bigger. When it comes to your business's growth, it depends on your commitment to learning—and learning is a deliberate action that takes effort and repetition and commitment, just as weightlifting does. It asks that you first admit you don't know something and then make a commitment to finding out as much as you can about whatever that thing is.

You notice I don't say *be taught, find training,* or *be trained.* Teaching and training are things that happen to you. Learning is something you choose to participate in. I say *yearn to learn.* To yearn means to seek after, to hunger for, to pursue it. As a leader, I can provide all the learning opportunities in the world for my people, but they must choose to want to learn.

The world today is full of opportunities to learn. With the access we have to the internet, there's no reason for any of us to be lacking knowledge. One way or another, we should be able to go out there and find the knowledge we need whenever we're faced with something we don't know or understand. Then we have to apply it—and that's another story.

WISDOM VERSUS KNOWLEDGE

There's a saying that goes like this: "Knowledge is knowing that a tomato is a fruit. Wisdom is not putting it into a fruit salad."

For almost twenty years of my life, I lived in Claremont, California, a city full of boutique colleges. In Claremont, academia rules. People have more letters after their names than most of us ever knew existed. Whenever I talked to these folks, I realized that, for them, pursuing knowledge was their highest value. They valued education not so that they could understand the world better or achieve something new, but because they thought of it as something they could accumulate, like money. The more knowledge they could have the better, even if it was the sort of knowledge they'd never be able to use in any practical sort of way.

In my opinion, that's a real waste of education. If we don't apply the knowledge we have in some way, out there in the real world, how does it serve us? What good is it? If it doesn't allow us to do our work better or contribute to the world in some larger way, what's the point of it? To sit around pontificating? I guess I'm too simple to see any value in that.

We need knowledge, of course we do. I'm all for education, and as leaders, we want to be sure we are constantly gaining all the knowledge we can. But knowledge alone isn't the same thing as wisdom. In my mind, wisdom means knowing how to apply the knowledge we have. It's making knowledge useful in concrete and visible ways.

A few years ago I was feeling frustrated with a sales department that just didn't seem to be going anywhere. Month after month, year after year, their numbers stayed the same. Finally, I went to the leader of the sales department, a guy named Jesse, with twenty years of sales experience. I asked him, "What's the last book you read?"

He kind of hemmed and hawed and, finally, admitted he couldn't remember the last time he'd read a book, any book. "Maybe back when I was in college?" he said.

I was blown away by his answer, but at least I knew what I needed to do next. We set up a reading program for the sales department, and we started them off with a book on manufacturing. "Why manufacturing?" Jesse asked. "Shouldn't we be reading about sales?"

"Guess what, Jesse," I said. "You sell manufactured products."

So they grumbled a little, but the sales department personnel started working through their reading list.

Before long, I was getting new feedback from our customers. Whenever I talk to customers, I always ask them a couple of questions: What do we do well? What do we need to improve? Now, all of sudden, I was hearing answers such as "Your salespeople are the foremost experts in this market," or "Your salespeople talk the same language we do. They talk like they're manufacturing people."

My salespeople were talking about efficiencies, made-to-order, and just-in-time inventory returns—all the buzzwords that were part of our customers' world. More importantly, though, my salespeople understood how these terms impacted our customers. They didn't just have new knowledge; they were able to apply their knowledge in practical ways. They had wisdom.

And guess what? Our sales went up. The stagnation I'd been seeing was gone forever.

Years ago, my dad gave me a plaque with a quotation from Calvin Coolidge. It hangs on my wall. "Nothing in this world," it reads, "can take the place of persistence. Talent will not: nothing is more common than unsuccessful men with talent. Genius will not; unrewarded genius is almost a proverb. Education will not: the world is full of educated derelicts. Persistence and determination alone are omnipotent." Some people may interpret these sentences differently from the way I do, but to me, "persistence and determination" are all about applying the knowledge we have, whatever it is and however much of it we have, to the real world. It's being willing to accept that you don't know what you need to know, being willing to learn, and finally, making your knowledge useful.

> *One learns from books and example only that*
> *certain things can be done. Actual learning requires*
> *that you do those things.*
> **FRANK HERBERT**

INTERNALIZE IGNORANCE

To me, the phrase *internalize ignorance* doesn't mean that we all settle for being a bunch of ignorant slobs. Formal education, however, can give us the illusion that we have become experts. We think we've learned all we need to know on a given subject. The Japanese have a word, *sho-shin*, that means "beginner's mind"—a mental state of openness to new information and perspectives. Thinking of ourselves as experts tends to close our minds to new knowledge, but when we regard ourselves as having a beginner's mind, we know we don't know everything we need to know. As we internalize that sense, we yearn to learn.

sho-shin

> *In the beginner's mind there are many possibilities.*
> *In the expert's mind there are few.*
> **—SUZUKI**

When I say that we need to yearn to learn, I'm not recommending that we all go sign up for a new degree program. I'm not even saying that we should create self-education programs based on reading and research. What I'm talking about here is a state of mind: yearning—a craving, a hunger, a driving force that is expressed in a multitude of ways.

We all know what it means to yearn for affection. We long for close relationships; it's something at the core of our being, a need that pushes us to form connections with other human beings. Without them, we feel dissatisfied, empty. We know that something is missing from our lives. Yearning for learning should have the same urgency and insistence within our hearts and minds.

> *Not all readers are leaders, but all*
> *leaders are readers.*
> **HARRY S. TRUMAN**

THE LEARNING LEADER

Learning isn't an optional activity for us leaders. We have to constantly expand our knowledge base, continually accelerate our learning, and consistently engage in a quest to learn—or we'll quickly be left behind by the other businesses out there.

Sometimes, business leaders come to talk to me when they find themselves in financial trouble. Their businesses are about to go under, and they're desperate. One of the first questions I always ask them is, "When was the last seminar you attended?"

"Oh gosh," they say, "I can't remember. I've been too busy."

When they say that, I know they've been operating on cruise control—and that will take them only so far. Sooner or later, we all reach a point in the journey where we have to actively engage in the demands of the road. When that happens, we're in trouble if we discover we don't have the knowledge to handle the challenges we face.

A yearning to learn needs to be imbedded in every corporate culture—and it has to begin with the leader. You can't demand that your employees attend workshops and seminars and ongoing courses if you're not doing those things too.

CREATING A CULTURE OF CONTINUOUS LEARNING

Imagine if you were to form a new organization—and then, ten years later, realized you still had the exact same brainpower you started with. No one wants that! Your knowledge base—and your understanding of how to apply that knowledge—should increase exponentially each year you're in business.

If you want to create a culture of continuous learning, you have to reward the people who do it. Some employees will be naturally driven to learn, but for many, it will be an entirely new concept. They assume that because they graduated from high school, college, or university, they have achieved all the learning they need. Your responsibility to people like that is to create a corporate culture that rewards them for going further, for learning new things in a process that never ends. As the leader, you need to build a system that rewards people, whether monetarily or through some form of recognition, for engaging in all sorts of learning activities, from reading groups to workshops to college-level classes.

I'm not here to tell you exactly how to do this. You need to find what works for your organization, but here are just a few of the ways in which I've created a culture of learning at my company:

- We have an online book club, and we pay people to read books. Once employees can demonstrate they've read a book, whether by taking a test or discussing it with their supervisor and proving that they've grasped the key concepts—and know how to apply them—they get a gift card.

- On the plant floor, when someone has learned and mastered a specific skill, his name is listed on a board that everyone can see. As the skills accumulate after his name, he feels a sense of pride and achievement.

- I refer to the training programs our company offers as a university. Employees voluntarily sign up for a class. This is a structured learning environment with a curriculum, set class times, and dedicated teachers.

- One of the best methods I've found to train employees in a new process is to have them watch someone else do it. They watch, they take notes, and they ask questions. We discuss their questions, and then we say, "Okay, we showed you. Now can you show us?" And we have them demonstrate the process, maybe ten times or for half a day, or maybe even for a full day, depending on the complexity of the process. When we see that they've mastered the task, we say to them, "Great job. Now here's Mary, and she's new too.

Can you show Mary how to do what you just learned?" By showing them, discussing it with them, watching them do it, and having them show someone else how to do it, we've completed the learning process.

Not every business leader realizes how important a corporate culture of learning can be. I recently spoke to another CEO who had a great business concept and succeeded in building a $12 million business. Now, however, things were nosediving—and what did he do? He decided not to invest in sending his managers to a seminar. Instead, he went out and bought a brand-new truck.

"Why would you do that?" I asked him.

"Well," he said, "that seminar would have cost me $5,000 per manager. I couldn't afford it."

All I could do was shake my head. "You went out and bought a truck that started depreciating the second you drove it off the dealer's lot. But, let me tell you right now, an educated member of your team doesn't depreciate. The value of a person like that goes up exponentially in value."

When I attend management meetings for our staff in China, I run into another form of resistance to a culture of learning. The people sitting around the table are all highly educated, extremely knowledgable people, but they sit there like college freshmen, notepads in front of them and pens in their hands, and they write down every single word that I speak. While I'm talking, they've got their heads down, writing furiously.

Now you might think that they're demonstrating beginners' minds, by assuming that every word that falls from my mouth is a piece of wisdom they need to record, but that's not the sort of beginner's mind I'm talking about. I want them to be engaged in what I'm saying. I want to ask them questions and have them figure out answers on their own. My job is to show them the path to follow; their job is to reach the conclusions that lie at the end of that path. Since that attitude isn't a part of their culture in China, it takes some effort on my part before they can understand what I want.

The March 20, 2013, issue of *Forbes* magazine published an article, titled "How Corporate Learning Drives Competitive Advantage," in which Josh Bersin had this to say about a corporate culture of learning:

Think about the history of companies like Nokia who lost their market to new competitors like Apple, or the many search companies who lost the search market to Google. These companies don't fail to innovate. They simply fail to learn. That is, their organizational culture likely did not tolerate being open to mistakes, the messy process of disruption, and the need to iterate and learn at the same time you operate. People who invent and innovate must not only be very capable technically, they must have the freedom to learn and share what they've learned in an open environment. In [our] research we found that some of the most important elements of "capability building" include creating a management culture which is open to mistakes, building trust, giving people time to reflect, and creating a value system around learning. Companies that adopt [a] learning culture significantly outperform their peers in innovation, customer service, and profitability.

TEACHING VERSUS LEARNING

I don't believe in teaching my employees. If I teach you something, it's something that happens to you. It's an external force put on you while you sit there, passively. Instead, I want to create an environment where people will naturally learn—and learning is active; it's something that you do for yourself, rather than something that's done to you.

I know from experience that when people hear they have to attend a training program, most of them feel as if they're back in elementary school. They don't want to sit in one more boring class. I remember when I was a worker, my boss would say, "Tomorrow you will all have to attend a safety training class"—and inside my head, I'd be groaning, *You gotta be kidding me! Another safety class?* Not only did I dread sitting through one more boring class, but I was also offended. *I know how to do my job, I'd be thinking. I'm smart enough not to stick my fingers into the saw blades.*

Employees don't feel the same about training sessions that are presented as opportunities to learn. When I talk about "training your employees," what I really mean is that you create opportunities for them to learn, internalize, and apply new knowledge, not only for altruistic reasons but also for purely practical ones. The more your employees learn, the more they will drive your entire organization forward. They'll help you increase your market share. You'll have higher revenues, be able to open new locations, and expand your operations around the globe.

> *Change is the end result of all true learning.*
> **LEO BUSCAGLIA**

LEARNING AND PROBLEM SOLVING

One of the phrases that is a part of my company's core philosophy is this: "Continuously solving root problems drives organizational learning." This means that our commitment to actively finding and solving problems is the very thing that drives learning within our organization.

When I sit down to lead a learning session with employees, I don't start out with a long lecture in which I try to impart all my great knowledge. Instead, I ask questions: What are the biggest challenges you're facing? What are the things that scare you right now at work? Are there things that seem unsafe to you?

Once I have answers to all those questions, I move on to the next question: What do you guys think we should do about these issues? At this point, it's their turn to start throwing out ideas. They come up with new ideas that could help us, and then we ask more questions. In the process, some ideas get shot down, but others become more and more clear as possible solutions to our problems.

At the end of all this, employees totally own the learning process. My job has been only to ask questions. They've found the answers all on their own.

Not every employee will be comfortable with this form of problem-solving. There will always be some folks who say, "Just tell me what to do!" Unfortunately, that's how most of us learned at school: The teacher told us what she wanted us to know, and then we were supposed to spit it back at her. Internalizing and applying the knowledge often got skipped altogether, meaning that our knowledge never sank into us deeply enough to become wisdom. We may have known that tomatoes were technically fruits, but we didn't know enough not to put them into fruit salads.

To build the culture you want, at first you'll have to intentionally recruit for people who are already on the same wavelength. They already yearn to learn, and that yearning is embedded in their habits and personalities. As your business grows, though, and a culture of learning becomes more ingrained, you'll be able to bring in new people and show them a new way of looking at learning.

Some business leaders are as reluctant to try this approach as their employees are. I've heard CEOs complain that doing things this way will slow down their business's, growth because it takes too much time. But, they're looking at the issue all wrong when they think like that.

You might be able to tell a group of people everything you want them to know in three hours, while it could take them three days to reach the same understanding on their own. But those three days are worth it. They've built a strong foundation for going forward, whereas if you'd pushed your staff faster than they were ready to go, you could find your organizational house crumbling around you. Growth always has to be built on an expanded knowledge base. It takes patience, I know, and that's not always an easy quality for a leader to have. But, if you were to skip any of the ten fundamentals I'm sharing with you in this book, don't skip this one! You can't overlook this one and still be a successful heir to the business throne, I guarantee you.

One of the resources for learning that I love is Flipboard. Flipboard functions similarly to Pandora, except that instead of creating personalized music lists, it creates a personalized aggregate of informational content from social networks, publishers, news feeds, and other websites, and presents it in a magazine format that allows users to "flip" through the articles. In thirty minutes a day on Flipboard, I'm able to learn a bunch of new things that trigger new ideas and help me grow. It's available for mobile devices for free via all major app stores or at www.flipboard.com.

Learning is not only essential to businesses and you, as a business leader, but is also absolutely vital to you as a human being. Personally, I know I will never have everything figured out, but that's okay. Because I yearn to learn and I believe in my ability to learn, I have a quiet self-confidence that I'll be okay. I can handle whatever problems come along. No matter what happens, I can figure it out.

My personal business goal is to build new leaders who autonomously identify and resolve issues daily. Imagine if more people were to yearn to learn to solve the problems in their lives instead of hoping the government or someone else will do it!

CHAPTER 9

THINK OF MONEY AS JUST A WAY TO KEEP SCORE

Imagine you are a football coach. It's the fourth quarter with one minute to go, and your team is down three points. What are you going to do? One thing I bet you *wouldn't* do is stand there staring at the scoreboard for those last three minutes, praying for the numbers to miraculously change.

You don't have to be a sports fan to know how silly that would be! The scoreboard isn't going to do anything all by itself. It's not alive. It doesn't have the capability of doing anything at all without human input, and even then, it's simply an indicator of what's going on in the field. If you're the coach and all you do is stare at the scoreboard, you're not doing your job.

A good coach would be so intently focused on the field that he'd instantly know how to use those last three minutes. He'd be calling out plays, changing out players, reading the defense as well as offense, and trying to move that ball into the end zone in whatever way he could. Maybe, he'd go for a field goal, or maybe he'd try a Hail Mary pass—and *then* the numbers on the scoreboard might change. The coach's skills and his intense focus on the game are the only things that could make different numbers appear. The scoreboard (money) represents the level at which we are executing on the field (our business).

MISSING THE GAME

Recently, I was talking to a businesswoman who is completely obsessed with a specific amount of money she wants to reach in sales. She has a single handmade product that she sells, and she's utterly determined she has to reach $110 million in sales in order to be successful. That number drives her. She's like the football coach who can't take his eyes off the scoreboard.

I wanted to give her some useful advice, so I suggested that she create a one-page business plan, followed up with an accountability plan. I thought if she had some tools to work with, she'd be able to get her focus back on the game, so I gave her some homework. But the next time I talked to her, she was still focused on that number of $110 million. In her mind, she had to achieve that amount of sales, no matter what. The problem is it's just a number. It doesn't mean anything unless it's attached to a game plan.

Finally, I asked her, "Why is $110 million so important to you? Where did you come up with that number?"

It turns that before her father died, he had the goal of making $100 million from his business. Meanwhile, this woman had always had her own financial goal, which was to make $10 million. When her father died without ever having reached his goal, she added on his number to hers: $110 million. It was an emotional commitment she'd made in memory of her father. But it had nothing to do with a business plan.

So I said to her, "Well, okay—but I'm not sure that's a good way to set a realistic financial goal for your company. $110 million is a lot of money. And you're selling products that cost $30 each. I'm not saying you can't do it. You can. But you're going to have to figure out a way to sell an awful lot of your product."

I still wasn't sure she understood what I was trying to tell her, so I pulled out the football analogy. "Listen," I said, "I never, ever had a football coach who told me I had to make sure I got a six up on the scoreboard. Instead, he showed me how to make the touchdown that would get that six up there on the board. He talked to me about tackling and blocking, about being quick on my feet during a key play. And when I did all those things, that's when the six appeared on the scoreboard. I didn't earn it by focusing on the number. I earned it by playing the game to the best of my ability."

"What are you saying?" she asked me.

"I'm saying that you've made up your mind you want a certain number up on the scoreboard—and you're so focused on that score that you're missing the game."

This businesswoman shouldn't feel stupid for being confused, because I know CEOs of multimillion-dollar companies who have made this same mistake. In fact, not too long ago, when I spoke to the managers of a franchise company that provides house-cleaning services, I heard them referring again and again to the dollar amount for their company's worth. All their discussions centered on making that number grow. Eventually, I stopped them and asked them to tell me the purpose of their business.

"To go into people's homes and provide cleaning services," was the answer.

"Okay," I said. "That's your product. That's the thing that you're selling. So don't you think you should be working on improving your product rather than focusing on how much money you are or aren't making? Shouldn't you be asking yourselves, 'What can we do to make customers trust our services? How can we better deliver those services? What are we doing right and what might we be doing wrong?'"

As many business leaders do, these guys knew they'd be judged on the basis of their financial reports, and they had forgotten about the real purpose of their business. It's easy to fall into the trap of focusing on the numbers and forgetting the game that's going on in front of you.

No matter what business you're in, money is not your goal. If you thought it was, then you're mistaken. And yes, I am aware of the famous book by Eli Goldrat that says money is the goal of the company . . . but I disagree. Money is just a way to keep score. Your goal is creating an environment where your people can do their absolute best! Your goal is operational excellence. It's learning to do what you do in the best possible way. Part of that will be knowing your financial data, but it won't be the end goal you're going for.

KNOW YOUR NUMBERS—BUT DON'T FOCUS ON THEM

Let me be clear here. I'm *not* saying that you should skip off into the rainbow and never think about money again. All organizations need money in order to exist. If a business *doesn't* make money, it's not going to last very long.

What's more, to lead a business, you have to know your numbers, inside out, from top to bottom. You can't make smart decisions if you're totally disregarding your available financial resources. In fact, there should never be a moment when you don't have an intimate and detailed knowledge of your financial data.

This means you have to demand that your accounting people give you accurate, timely, financial reports, and once you get them, no matter how much red is on them, you have to study them. If you don't analyze those red numbers because they're depressing or they scare you, you're just putting your head in the sand.

Whenever I mentor other business leaders, one of the things I ask about is their latest financial report.

All too often, they say something like, "Oh, I haven't looked at it yet."

And then I say, "What do you mean you haven't looked at it?"

"Yeah," they say, "I got it two or three weeks ago, but I haven't had a chance to look at it."

"You haven't had a chance to look at it?" I shake my head in disbelief.

Scoreboards have a purpose. They tell you if you're executing properly on the field. If you're not, you need to know, so you can take corrective action. And you need to keep track of your financials for that same reason. You need to look at them, and you need to be able to understand the story they tell you. If there's a blip in your business's performance, it's going to show up in those reports—and that allows you to fix the problem before the blip turns into a major issue.

Keep in mind that numbers are never merely numbers. Every line in your financial report represents a person, a product, or a process. Understanding the real meaning of the report requires your full engagement with your entire business. Looking at financial reports is not a behind-the-desk activity; it's a manage-by-walking-around (MBWA) task.

Say you see that your sales numbers are 7 percent lower than last year. You can sit at your desk all day long asking why, but you'll never find the answer until you go to the sales department and find out what they're doing—or not doing—this year. The Japanese call this *gemba*. It means going to where the work is performed and seeing what is going on.

Or what if there's a number you don't understand? The only way you'll find the answer is by asking the appropriate department staff, "What's this? And why does it cost so much more this quarter than it did last quarter?"

Something very similar to this happened to me one day as I was looking at a financial report. I noticed a massive increase in costs, so I went to my purchasing department and asked, "What's going on here? Why are these numbers so high?"

"Because the cost of wood nearly doubled," I was told.

"Oh," I said. "Well, what do we do about it?"

Everyone stared at me. No one said a word.

"Should we put it out to get bids from other vendors?" I asked.

"Well, we really like this vendor," someone said. "He's just such a great guy."

"Okay." I stared back at them for a moment. "This great guy just doubled the cost of one of our main component parts. Does his increase represent what the rest of the market is doing? What's going on here?"

No one knew the answer—but they found out. And they wouldn't have if I hadn't been matching up financial reports to real-life circumstances. Now, that was a symptom of a deeper problem that required me to work with the purchasing department to "see the whole."

The money scoreboard allows you to spot problems, track them down to their source, and find solutions. You won't be able to do that without intimate knowledge of your financial data. You cannot stick your head in the sand, because when you don't attend to problems, they don't get better. If you slap a Band-Aid over a small infected cut, you won't have to look at it, but covering it up isn't going to make it better. In fact, when you pull the Band-Aid off, it's going to be substantially worse. What started out as a tiny cut that might have healed very quickly can end up as deadly gangrene—and the same sort of thing can happen with your business.

Understanding and being aware of your financial numbers is not the same thing as making them your goal; however, they're an indication of your performance. Knowing them can help you reach your goal, but they're not the goal itself. When they indicate a problem, it's like putting a thermometer in your mouth and discovering that you have a fever of 102. The number doesn't *make* you sick, but it does let you know that you are sick. Now you can take steps to address your illness so that you feel better. No one would say, "My overall goal for my health is to keep my temperature at 98.6." Numbers are useful, but in the end, they're only numbers.

There may, of course, be short periods of time when it may make sense to focus on the numbers until you get them high enough to give your company stability. But for the long term, focusing on finances is not a sustainable model. You'll burn out. I can guarantee it. When life's storms come along, the clouds will hide the scoreboard from view. With nothing to focus on, you'll say to yourself, "This isn't worth it." And it won't be. Ultimately, no number, no matter how large it is, can justify all your hard work.

Making operational excellence your focus is a much more sustainable vision. It has staying power that will get you through the dark days. It's also a vision that will cascade down throughout an organization, making people feel glad to be a part of something that constantly strives for excellence in its field.

> *A wise person should have money in their head,*
> *but not in their heart.*
> **JONATHAN SWIFT**

THE PRACTICAL PERSPECTIVE

You could look at it from the motivational viewpoint—what will keep you working for the next five or ten or thirty years?—but you can also look at it from a purely practical perspective. If you want higher scores, then you need to focus on the game. When you concentrate on the quality of your business, you become more successful and make more money. It's as simple as that.

If you, as the leader, overemphasize the numbers, you inevitably create a corporate culture that's also focused on dollar signs. That means there's a whole bunch of you staring at the scoreboard. But who's taking care of your customers? No one.

Former Goldman Sachs Executive Director Greg Smith had realized this about his company when he decided to resign because, he wrote in a March 14, 2012, *New York Times* op-ed, "the interests of the client continue to be sidelined in the way the firm operates and thinks about making money." He went on to say:

> It might sound surprising to a skeptical public, but culture
> was always a vital part of Goldman Sachs's success. It
> revolved around teamwork, integrity, a spirit of humility,
> and always doing right by our clients. The culture was the
> secret sauce that made this place great and allowed us to

earn our clients' trust for 143 years. It wasn't just about making money; this alone will not sustain a firm for so long . . . I am sad to say that I look around today and see virtually no trace of the culture that made me love working for this firm for many years.

Smith challenged Goldman Sachs' executives to "make the client the focal point of your business again," and warned:

Without clients you will not make money. In fact, you will not exist. Weed out the morally bankrupt people, no matter how much money they make for the firm. And get the culture right again, so people want to work here for the right reasons. People who care only about making money will not sustain this firm—or the trust of its clients—for very much longer.

If you, as the leader of your business, talk about customers only as a means to put a number up on that scoreboard, that attitude will trickle down to your employees. When people no longer care about customers but, instead, just want to make money off them, they forget about operational excellence. They stop caring about the quality of the product they're making. When that happens, it's only a matter of time before the customers start to feel it—and decide to take their business elsewhere.

Again, let me repeat, I'm not saying that making a profit isn't important. You can't pay employees and you can't serve customers without a healthy bottom line. But when you make dollar signs your sole purpose, it's only a matter of time before your customers figure you out. And at that point, your focus on the numbers is going to work against you; it's going to make your score lower than it would have been if you'd had your eye on the game (and customers are an important part of that game).

> *You can only become truly accomplished at something you love. Don't make money your goal. Instead, pursue the things you love doing, and then do them so well that people can't take their eyes off you.*
> **MAYA ANGELOU**

MY STORY

If you intently focus on that game and put all your drive into perfect execution, I promise you at the end of the game, you'll look up and that scoreboard is going to blow your mind. How do I know this? Because that's what happened to me.

I never, ever dreamed I'd be as successful as I am today. I don't only mean that I wouldn't have believed it was possible that one day I'd be a multimillionaire. I mean that it never even crossed my mind. It just wasn't a goal I had for myself. It wasn't something that was important to me.

I started my professional career when I was eighteen years old, working for a printing company. The owner, a guy named Gene, who was twenty-nine years old (to me, he seemed ancient), treated me as though I were an adult. I put on slacks and a button-down shirt with a tie, and I went out to sell printing to small businesses in Orange County.

At that point in my life, Gene represented success. He had a nice business, a nice home, and he made around a million dollars a year in gross sales. The longer I worked for him, the more I started thinking that, maybe, I could be like Gene. I could do okay in business. I could even be a success. If someone had asked me at that point in my life, "Aaron, make a prediction. Where do you think you're going to be, financially, in twenty years?" I would have taken a look at the "scoreboard" and come up with my best estimate of what the score was going to be later in the game. Here's what I would have said: "I'll be making $150,000 a year. I hope I'll own a small boat and a nice house."

If I had set that scoreboard prediction in my mind and focused on it, I'm pretty sure that's all I would have accomplished. I might not have even achieved that much. Instead, though, I never gave the scoreboard too much thought. I was more excited about learning new things and growing. Once I had my own business, I was focused on making it the best possible business it could be. I never had a hard and fast idea of how much money I wanted to make. I never believed I had to get to X number of dollars. I asked how we could do better, become more efficient, and make the work easier. What did our customers want? What did our customers need? How could we blow their minds? I was so busy finding the answers to those questions that I didn't think much at all about the scoreboard.

And then, one day, as I was flying in my personal jet, it suddenly hit me. "What am I doing?" I asked myself. "How did I get here?" I was a hundred times more successful than I could have predicted back when I was eighteen.

I can't guarantee that your story will be the same as mine. But I do know that when you focus on what your business does and you become proficient at it—and then you become excellent at it—the scoreboard will reflect your effort. The numbers you see will be bigger than you ever dreamed.

> *A business that makes nothing but money*
> *is a poor business.*
> **HENRY FORD**

CHAPTER 10

PAY ATTENTION TO FOUR THINGS—AND DELEGATE THE REST

I like to take care of my employees. So much so, in fact, that I used to go to Costco myself to pick up snacks and sodas to stock the employee kitchen. As I pushed the cart down the aisle, I'd be thinking what a great CEO I was. I was taking care of my people, getting yummy snacks for them—and sodas—and coffee. *And how about some candy? That looks good. They'll like that.* I'd smile to myself, thinking all the time, *Look at me. I'm such a kind and caring boss.*

One day, though, one of my drivers said something to me that wiped that smug smile right off my face. "Sir," he said, "I don't know how much you make an hour, but I'm sure it's a lot more than the sixteen dollars an hour I make. If you give me a list, I could go to Costco and pick those things up. Wouldn't that be a better use of the company's funds?"

He was absolutely right, of course. Here I was trying to prove what a humble guy I was by doing the shopping at Costco, and all the while, what I was really doing was costing the organization. Everybody in the company saw it but me.

If you've been placed in a position of leadership, you have accountability for the lives of other human beings, and that's a tremendous responsibility. Your decisions will shape their families' opportunities, their health, their old age, and their ability to contribute to the entire community in meaningful ways. Like it or not, their lives are in your hands. The more seriously you take this responsibility, the more it will drive you to be a great leader, someone who is truly capable of being the heir to the throne. But, sometimes the weight of all this can seem nearly too heavy to bear. Whenever I start to feel that way, I remember the mistake I made when I thought I needed to do the shopping at Costco. I take a good look at myself, and often, I'll find that I've taken on more responsibility than I need to.

There are only four things we leaders need to focus on. Whether we have three employees or three thousand, those four things are the same:

1. people and culture,

2. sales,

3. financial data, and

4. our market.

That's it. Anything else should be done by someone else in our organization.

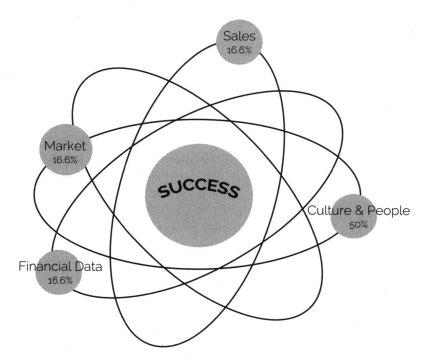

This diagram represents the leader's ideal workday: 50 percent of work hours spent on people and culture, and the remaining 50 percent divided among understanding sales, financial data, and the market.

PEOPLE AND CULTURE

If you're the leader of a business, you should plan on spending 50 percent of your time on building your culture with your people. This means if you work ten hours a day, then five hours out of every day should be spent on this. Think of yourself as the chief human resource manager.

There's a reason we talk about *human resources*. As we said in Chapter 5, human beings are the greatest resource a business has. Imagine that your business is a game of chess. You wouldn't want to have all pawns, but you also wouldn't want to have only a queen. Each of the chess pieces has different skills, and each and every one of them is important. Without them, there's no game. And, without your employees, you don't have a business. They need to be your first and greatest focus.

Part of your focus on your people will involve building a strong culture. We talked about how to create a corporate culture in Chapter 1, so I'm not going to repeat myself here. But, I will suggest that you try an exercise that's loosely based on one Jim Collins outlines on his website, www.jimcollins.com.

Imagine you've been asked to build a branch of your company on another planet, but there are only five seats on the spaceship. Whom would you send? If you wanted to recreate your company far away from home, you would need to pick the five people who best embodied your business. You'd want these people to not only have the skills to build the business but also the necessary beliefs and values.

Now ask yourself what values these five people bring to their work. What are their most fundamental characteristics? You can probably answer these questions without consulting the individuals themselves, but most likely, they'll need to answer the following three questions for you: Which of your values do you think will be just as important a hundred years from now as they are today? Would you still hold these values even if it meant you had to sacrifice income? If you were to start over at a new company, which values would you bring with you, even if you were in an entirely different line of work?

At the end of this exercise, you should have a pretty good idea of your company's core values. You didn't create these values. You didn't spend hours coming up with them on your own. No, these are the core values that are already embedded in your company's DNA. Now your job is to nurture them. Half of your time as the business leader should be spent building those values into the daily structure of your company.

You need to do this if you have only a handful of employees, but it becomes even more important the larger you grow. Those values are the foundation that will keep your business solid. If you try to build a huge corporation without them, eventually the business will crumble. It won't survive.

The side of the business trail is littered with the dead bodies of companies whose people thought they could make it without foundational core values. They may have made the journey just fine so long as the sun was shining and everything was going well. Once the storms hit, though—and storms always come along, sooner or later—these businesses came apart at the seams. They couldn't keep going. They eventually dropped down dead. I'm sure you'll recognize most of the names on the gravestones over their bodies, names like Enron, Blockbuster, and Sears.

Meanwhile, businesses that build cultures centered on core values are thriving. Zappos is a good example of this. CEO Tony Hsieh believed that if he could get his culture right, everything else would fall into place. So, Zappos didn't just make a list of pretty-sounding values and post them in the faculty lunchrooms. Instead, they built their values into their hiring practices. They discovered that a lot of smart, talented people were too egotistical to align with Zappos' values—so those people didn't get hired. Hsieh absolutely believes that culture is what will make his company successful in the long term. Southwest Airlines is another example of a company that has incorporated its values into its hiring process. This ensures that they hire only friendly, enthusiastic people—and Southwest Airlines has been consistently profitable for more than forty years.

While creating hiring standards that center on your core values is essential to maintaining the corporate culture you want, you can go further than that. The more you are engaged with your employees, praising them, reprimanding them, awarding bonuses and raises, all based on your company's core values, the more you will reinforce that structure. Every single discussion you have with employees should always come back to your core values.

Spending 50 percent of your time on this may seem counterintuitive. You may think you're way too busy with other things to carve out so much time for your people and your culture, but I promise you, this is an absolutely essential commitment you need to make. At first, you'll have to make it an intentional thing you remind yourself to do daily, but eventually, it will become ingrained in how you think about your job.

> *No company, small or large, can win over the long run without energized employees who believe in the mission and understand how to achieve it.*
> **JACK WELCH**

PAY ATTENTION TO SALES

If half your time is spent on your people and culture, that leaves the other half to be divided up into three parts. This means that you'll be devoting about 16.6 percent of your time on each of them. Out of a ten-hour workday, you'll spend a little more than an hour and a half on each of them, and the first of these is sales.

As the company's leader, you need to know your sales process backward and forward. How do people consume your product—and why? What drives them? What do your customers want?

If you don't know the answers, how can you help your business grow? You can't. And yet, sometimes, I hear executives say, "I'm just not a sales person. That's not where my skills lie." When I talk to them further, I realize they have no idea how their company's revenue stream comes in. I always think, *Well, you've got a problem. You'd better develop some sales skills if you want to succeed.*

I don't care what business you're in. You'd better know how to sell your product. In fact, if you're the owner or CEO of a business, you'd better be the best sales person you have. You should believe in your product or service more than anyone else. You should be totally convinced that it will change the world, enrich lives, and deliver more quality than any similar product or service out there. You should be excited about it, passionate about it, constantly talking about it.

Your customers may not know yet that they need what you have to offer—but you know. This is another time when you can't make money your goal, because if you do, you won't have any credibility as a sales person. You need to be absolutely convinced that your product or service will improve people's lives in ways they may not even suspect.

This means you can't simply go out there and ask consumers what they want. They actually may not know. There's a quotation from Henry Ford that I refer to often: "Had I asked my customers what they wanted, they would have told me a faster horse." Customers don't always know how to think past what they already know. If companies were to base their approach to product development only on what customers thought they wanted, we'd be still using rotary phones, watching black-and-white televisions, and listening to all our music on vinyl records.

I'm not saying that product development is one of the four things you need to pay attention to as a business leader. You should, however, understand your customers better than they understand themselves—and then, with both passion and integrity, give them not what they want but what they truly need. As author Nelson Boswell has said, "Here is the simple but powerful rule—always give people more than they expect to get."

> *I have found no greater satisfaction than achieving success through honest dealing and strict adherence to the view that, for you to gain, those you deal with should gain as well.*
> **ALAN GREENSPAN**

UNDERSTAND YOUR FINANCIAL DATA

Once you understand sales, you'll be able to connect it to your financial reports. Financial data needs to occupy the next 16.6 percent of your time. You need to understand how all the moving parts of your business impact your financial well-being. The importance of this goes back to your 50 percent focus on your people. You need to be able to milk every last dollar to provide opportunities for your employees to grow and advance.

Do you have accurate, timely, clean, trustworthy financials? Do you get them on a regular basis? Would you bet the lives of your children on that financial data? That makes it a very, very high standard, I know, but if you think about it, you are betting the well-being of your employees' children on those numbers. Your decisions will impact each one of your employees and their families, so you better be darn sure you're working from accurate numbers.

In Chapter 9, I told you that money is just a way to keep score, and that's true. Don't do things for money. Money is the result of doing a good job in the day-to-day execution of your business. It's not the goal, it's the score, but that score needs to be reliable, and you need to understand what it means. If a football coach looked up at the scoreboard and didn't understand whether the numbers meant that his team were winning or losing, he'd be a pretty poor coach!

> *When it comes to money, ignorance is NOT bliss.*
> *What you don't know CAN hurt you.*
> **SANDRA S. SIMMONS**

KNOW YOUR MARKET

The last slice of your time, accounting for about 16.6 percent of every workday, should be devoted to understanding what's going on in your marketplace. This connects directly to sales and financial data in obvious ways. Keep in mind that it has nothing to do with production or order entry, or any of the other tactical issues that aren't one of your four core focuses. Someone else can take care of those things just fine, so long as you are using your time correctly, but you, as the leader, need to understand your marketplace so that you can identify opportunities for your business—and your employees—to grow.

GEMBA

I like to call our marketplace the sandbox. It's where we play—and it's where your customers also play; it's where they interact with your product or service. You need to go out there and see where your product or service is being used or consumed.

Let's say the service you offer is medical billing for doctors' offices. You need to physically visit these offices so that you can find out what they really need. What challenges are they facing? How could you make their lives easier for them? What trends are happening in their field? What are their typical budgets? What do their IT systems look like? Is your service easily compatible with their existing software and electronic processes?

Or imagine you make dental crowns for dentists' offices. If you're going to know your marketplace, you'd better be talking not only to dentists but also to their patients. Are the people who just got a crown happy with the way your product looks? Do they like the way it feels? What's their biggest complaint? You won't know the answers to questions like these unless you're out there in the sandbox.

The word I use for this concept is the Japanese term *gemba* (real thing, real place), which I mentioned earlier. It's a concept that stresses direct observation of what's going on in the real world. In other words, it's not about abstract discussions that go on in some boardroom. Gemba is all about interacting, in person, with the places and people that affect your business.

Gemba can be applied to other aspects of your business, but when it comes to the marketplace, it means that, as the leader, you'll need to go to your customers' place of business or lifestyle, where you'll be able to see (with your actual eyes) and listen (with your physical ears) to the customers' problems and opportunities. When you engage in gemba, you're gathering and processing data, but you're using your own five senses to do so. It's also a form of MBWA (management by walking around), because it asks that you get up from your chair, leave your office, and go see what's really happening out there.

The Japanese characters for *gemba* mean, literally, "the king looking out under the hot sun at the land where the pigs are." The king could have sent an overseer to check on the pigs, but he went himself so that he would have direct, sensory knowledge of the condition of his pigs.

NETWORKING

Another part of understanding your marketplace involves networking. In today's global world, no business is a silo standing all by itself. Things that are happening in other parts of the globe will affect every business everywhere. Even if you're a tiny company with five employees, something can happen half a world away that has a direct impact on you and your business. Currency movements and changes in commodity prices are only two of the more obvious ways the global economy impacts local businesses. The only way you can keep up with the enormity of this is to be an active part of a network that keeps you informed.

This means you'll be talking to your banker, your lawyer, your accountant. You might want to join a trade organization, or a CEO group, which can be an incredibly helpful investment of your time and money. Examples of CEO groups are the Renaissance Forum, Vistage, and Venwise. Believe me, as a business leader, I know how lonely it can be, sometimes, sitting in that chair, but there's no reason to bear the burden all alone when you can join a group of other people who are facing the same challenges you are. When you meet once a month, you can pool your perspectives on the market, and the other members of your group may be able to point out something important that you've missed. (Going back to Chapter 8, CEO groups are also tremendous opportunities for learning.)

Another way to build your network is to go to your industry's tradeshows. These are great opportunities to connect with people who are in the same business you are. You can walk around the floor and get a good idea of what other people are doing. Even better, most tradeshows offer seminars and workshops where you'll be able to learn and connect more directly. You might want to volunteer to speak at one of these workshops because networking also means letting other people get to know you and interact with the perspectives you have to offer.

All of these activities will help you to better understand your market. As human beings, our personal perspectives are unavoidably limited. The only way to compensate for that is by being a part of an active, widespread network that will feed you information and viewpoints you wouldn't, otherwise, be able to see.

> *Networking is marketing. Marketing yourself, marketing your uniqueness, marketing what you stand for.*
> **CHRISTINE COMAFORD-LYNCH**

BE CURIOUS

The third method of focusing on your market is by feeding your curiosity. (Again, this has a lot to do with yearning to learn, as we talked about in Chapter 8.) In other words, have an insatiable curiosity about what makes your customers tick. What interests them? What do they need? What new idea would enrich their lives?

The best way to feed your curiosity is by consuming content. Read books and magazines and watch movies. Don't just consume content that's in your area of expertise, but read about ideas and events outside the scope of your business. Be open to new ideas that could trigger another idea that might be exactly what your market needs.

I got into the jet charter business, for example, because of an article I read on Flipboard. The story was about a guy whose business owned a couple of airplanes. When his business took a downturn, he could no longer afford the planes. Instead of looking at them as liabilities, though, he saw them as resources, and he was able to build a successful charter airplane business in Europe. *That's interesting*, I thought, and then my mind went to the two corporate jets I owned. *What if . . . ?*

So be curious. Wonder constantly about what's going on in the world. Ask questions, look for answers, don't make assumptions, and have the beginner's mind we talked about in Chapter 8.

> *I have no special talents. I am only passionately curious.*
> **ALBERT EINSTEIN**

KNOW YOUR DEMOGRAPHICS

To understand your market, you have to know the demographics contained within it. This is especially important if your business is expanding, opening up new branches in new cities or in different countries. You can't assume that what works in one location will work everywhere!

I started out with a factory in the United States. When I opened one in China, I expected it to have most of the same challenges and strengths as my American factory did. Let me tell you. It was not at all the same! As I told you back in Chapter 5, it was hard work to embed our DNA in the factory in China (and I couldn't have done it without Angel).

The next factory I opened was in Mexico. This time, I assumed that because I had lots of Hispanic employees at my American plant, I wouldn't have the learning curve we had in China. I thought that since I understood Hispanic culture, it would be a piece of cake to get the Mexican factory up and running.

I sent down a management team of twenty Mexican American workers from my American factory to open the Mexican facility. After only a month, my managers were beside themselves. I went down to see what was going on and found that they were furious with the Mexican workers. "They're lazy!" they told me. "They don't know how to come to work on time. They don't know how to work." One manager said, "Let me tell you right now, these Mexicans, they're not like us."

I'd made a big mistake. I didn't understand the sandbox we were playing in. The culture in Mexico is very different from the culture in the United States, and ethnic background doesn't change that. The same differences we were seeing in the workers also existed in the marketplace, and I needed to understand them if I wanted us to be successful in Mexico.

The story I like to tell my employees is about Kraft's Oreo cookies when they went to China in 1996. Oreos are Americans' favorite cookie, so Kraft assumed that the Chinese would like them too. What's not to like?

Now everyone knows what an Oreo cookie is like—flat and round, black and white, and intensely sweet. It's been that way for a hundred years. Why mess with perfection? But Oreos turned out to not be such a big hit in China. Kraft came close to pulling them out but then decided to do some research. So, the company went to customers and asked what was wrong with an Oreo cookie.

Well, it turned out that people who hadn't grown up with Oreos thought they were weird-tasting little things—a little too bitter and a little too sweet, all at the same time. Also, the Chinese don't drink milk much, so the thought of dunking a cookie in milk didn't make much sense to them. And then, the whole thing of twisting the top off and licking the cream out—again, not something they grew up with, so it was a strange concept for them. Who wants to take apart their cookies before they eat them?

So, Kraft changed the recipe for their Chinese market and made the wafers a little sweeter and the cream less sweet.

"That's better," the Chinese consumers said, and Oreos began to sell a whole lot more in China.

Now that the folks at Kraft had opened their minds to new possibilities, they decided to go even further. If nothing was sacrosanct about Oreos, then they could change everything in order to appeal to the Chinese market. Now Oreos no longer had to be black and white, so they could have a green-tea filling. Or, they could have a bright orange filling between mango- and orange-flavored wafers.

Then, Kraft took its willingness to change even further. Why does an Oreo have to be flat and round? Why couldn't it be shaped like a straw, with the dark part on the outside and the white cream on the inside of the tube? When Kraft did that, Oreo sales doubled, and then doubled again, and then again. Now it's the best-selling cookie in China.

Many fast food restaurants have also done a good job of adjusting their product to different market demographics. McDonald's, for example, has created the following foods that would probably never fly in the United States but do really well in the market where they're being sold:

If Kraft could think outside the box enough to make an Oreo that looks like this, what could you do to adapt your product or service to new markets?

- People in China love McDonald's taro pie. It has the same crispy shell as the classic McDonald's apple pie, but it's stuffed with bright purple taro root instead of apple.

- In India, people stop into McDonald's for a McCurry Pan— curried vegetables baked in a cream sauce inside a crispy "pan" that's made from bread. The all-vegetarian versions of McDonald's were first installed along religious pilgrimage routes in India, and then spread from there.

- The Japanese like the McDonald's Shrimp Filet-O, a burger of panko-battered shrimp, topped with tempura sauce and lettuce.

Don't assume that your product couldn't be adapted for new regions too. Do some research and get to know the demographics—and then be willing to think outside the box. Smash your preconceptions. Have a beginner's mind about your product or service. Who knows what you might come up with!

> *Authentic marketing is not the art of selling what you make but knowing what to make. It is the art of identifying and understanding customer needs and creating solutions that deliver satisfaction to the customers.*
>
> **PHILIP KOTLER**

DELEGATE

So there you have it, the only four things you should be focusing on as the heir to the throne: people and culture, sales, financial data, and your market. Don't make the job more complicated than it has to be. Focus on those four things and leave the rest to your employees.

It sounds simple, but many leaders, including me, have found it hard to delegate. I've heard a whole lot of excuses (and I've said some of them myself): I'm too busy to delegate. It's faster if I just do things myself, or I'm the only one who knows how to do this thing right. Everyone else messes it up. An excuse that most leaders would be unwilling to voice out loud is that they're afraid they'll lose their sense of importance or be upstaged if they pass along important work to their employees. They like feeling they're the go-to expert in certain areas, and they hoard their knowledge. Another reason why leaders can find it difficult to delegate is that they're control freaks. They feel the need to micromanage, because letting someone else do the work feels like a loss of control.

But here's the truth: One of your most important tasks is to teach people how to think and ask the right questions so that they're capable of doing whatever task you give them. That's not something extra you have to fit into your already busy day. It's part of the 50 percent of your day that you've devoted to people and culture. Delegation should be integrated into your staff development.

It's also a whole lot easier to delegate when you know and trust your people and the culture of excellence that supports them. When you know your staff, you'll know who has the skills and motivation to do a job well. Accept your own limitations. Focus on being a good leader, and let your people learn and grow to new heights of responsibility and performance.

Andrew Carnegie, the steel tycoon who was the richest man of his day, once said, "No person will make a great business who wants to do it all himself or get all the credit." The inscription carved on his tombstone reflects his lifelong belief in delegation: "Here lies a man who knew how to enlist the service of better men than himself."

CONCLUSION

GREATNESS IS A PATH

When my son told me he wanted to learn to be the heir to the throne, I realized that when I started out, there was no one to tell me those things. I had to piece them together, little by little, year by year. I learned what I needed to know from a thousand different books and seminars and workshops—and from trying and failing and trying again.

This book is meant to be a guidebook for anyone who is hoping to be heir to the throne, in any sense of the word. It won't do the work for you. It's not a get-rich-quick book, and it doesn't have any magic formulas. You'll have to learn a whole lot on your own, just as I did. But, what I hope I've given you are ten big fundamentals that will point you in the right direction, year after year after year, for as long as you're in business.

1. Embrace culture first.

2. Continually improve.

3. Be loyal.

4. Enjoy hard work.

5. Actions speak louder than words.

6. Respect others.

7. Love change.

8. Yearn to learn.

9. Think of money as just a way to keep score.

10. Pay attention to just four things—and delegate the rest.

These ten fundamentals aren't actually separate to-do items on your life's list. To achieve greatness, you must define yourself by all ten. They're all connected, creating a mesh, a network that relies on all the others in order to work. You can't be willing to constantly improve if you don't love change. If you yearn to learn, you'll constantly improve. If, as a leader, your actions speak louder than your words, you'll inspire your employees to follow your example. And if you create a corporate culture where all of these traits are not only valued but also become habits, they'll be ingrained in your DNA. You can't pull out one item and do that first, because each of them connects to all the others.

But if I had to put my finger on one final key to my success, I would say that it's relentless **dissatisfaction**. I am never satisfied to stay in one place. I am never satisfied that I know all I need to know. I am never satisfied that we have done our best. It's this relentless dissatisfaction that has pushed me forward in life more than anything else, and that's the umbrella over everything I've said in this book, because each of the ten topics we've talked about are all part of my relentless dissatisfaction.

Being competitive isn't what got me where I am today. I don't judge myself against other companies. I don't even care what those companies are doing, and I don't care what the industry standard is. I only care about being better this year at what we do than we were last year—and being even better than that next year.

So, when I think about what I want my son or daughters to learn, more than anything else, I hope they'll gain that sense that they can always do better. There's always room to grow. There is always something new to learn. And, there are always new ways to inspire and challenge the people we lead.